COWBOY

The Illustrated History

COWBOY

The Illustrated History

Richard W. Slatta, Ph.D.

Sterling Publishing Co., Inc.
New York

Edited by J. E. Sigler
Designed by Eddie Goldfine
Layout by Gala Pre Press Ltd.

Special thanks from the author are given to R. Matthew Poteat, North Carolina State University graduate history student, for crucial research assistance.

The publisher warmly thanks Donald W. Reeves, McCasland Chair of Cowboy Culture, and the staff of the Donald C. & Elizabeth M. Dickinson Research Center, National Cowboy & Western Heritage Museum, for taking time out of their busy schedule to assist in researching photographic material for this project. We also thank Bill Barnhart and the team at OKC West Livestock Market Inc., as well as Mark Squires at the Express Ranches for their help.

Library of Congress Cataloging-in-Publication Data

Slatta, Richard W., 1947-
Cowboy: the illustrated history / Richard W. Slatta
p. cm.
Includes index.
ISBN 1-4027-1800-4
1. Cowboys-West (U.S.)-History. 2. Cowboys-West (U.S.)-History-Pictorial
2. Ranch life-West (U.S.) –History 4. Ranch life-West (U.S.)-History-Pictorial works.
5. West (U.S.)-Social life and customs. 6. West (U.S.)-Social life and customs-Pictorial works. 7. Cowboys-History. 8. Cowboys-History-Pictorial works. I. Title.

F596.S58 2006
978-dc22   2005051745

Library of Congress Cataloging-in-Publication Data

2   4   6   8   10   9   7   5   3   1

Published by Sterling Publishing Co., Inc.
387 Park Avenue South, New York, NY 10016
© 2006 Penn Publishing Ltd.
Distributed in Canada by Sterling Publishing
c/o Canadian Manda Group, 165 Dufferin Street
Toronto, Ontario, Canada M6K 3H6
Distributed in the United Kingdom by GMC Distribution Services
Castle Place, 166 High Street, Lewes, East Sussex, England BN7 1XU
Distributed in Australia by Capricorn Link (Australia) Pty. Ltd.
P.O. Box 704, Windsor, NSW 2756, Australia

Printed in China
All rights reserved

Sterling ISBN-13: 978–1-4027-1800-7
ISBN-10: 1-4027-1800-4

For information about custom editions, special sales, premium and corporate purchases, please contact Sterling Special Sales Department at 800-805-5489 or specialsales@sterlingpub.com.

Texas-born and Oklahoma-raised
J. W. Beeson well described the cowboy
in his 1989 poem "Last of a Breed":

He's one of the highly exalted,

In love with the life that he leads;

*He's known as a cowboy, a wild
buckeroo,*

A hero in legend and deed—

He's one of the Last of a Breed.

I dedicate this book to the many
generations of cowboys and other ranch
folk, the strong men and women who built
the Western cattle industry. May your heirs
continue to perpetuate ranch life and
cowboy culture!

Rich Slatta
The Cowboy Professor
Lazy S Ranch
Cary, North Carolina USA
January 2006

CONTENTS

Pages 4–5: *Jack Rhodes on his horse in a blizzard at Pitchfork (Timber Creek) Meeteetsee, Wyoming, circa 1926–1927.*

Page 6: *Cowboy with gun and wooly chaps. Unknown photographer, circa 1910.*

Page 7: *Elmer on horse in lake. Photographed by Charles J. Belden.*

Opposite: *Six cowboys in group portrait. Unknown photographer, circa 1890.*

The *Texas Live Stock Journal* (Fort Worth, October 21, 1882) wrote admiringly of the cowboy's courage, chivalry, and loyalty, comparing him to "the famed knights of old." Cowboys might be a bit short on "ball room etiquette, but no set of men have loftier reverence for women, and no set of men would risk more in the defense of their person or their honor." Lauding the cowboy's "entire devotion to the interests of his employer," the journal confidently declared: "We are certain no more faithful employee ever breathed than he."[1] Even allowing for a bit of journalistic hyperbole, it is clear that the cowboy of old inspired great reverence in his observers.

Yet the image of the cowboy has always been a two-sided coin. While some think of him as the tough, virtuous, straight-talking hero of the American West, others prefer to imagine him as a lawless, wild, shoot-'em-up villain that spread mayhem and chaos along the frontier. Even in his own day, the cowboy often became the victim of the ignorant calumny of outsiders, the press, and politicians, who vilified cowboys as reckless, violent, and uncivilized. The *Rio Grande Republican* (Las Cruces, New Mexico, December 13, 1884) offered a typically critical view of the cowboy, emphasizing his supposed tendency toward violence: "Out in the Territories there are only two classes—the 'cowboys' and the 'tenderfeet.' Such of the 'cowboys' as are not professional thieves, murderers and miscellaneous blacklegs who fled to the frontier for reasons that require no explanation, are men who totally disregard all of the amenities of Eastern civilization, brook no restraint, and—fearing neither God, nor man or the devil—yielding allegiance to no law save their own untamed passions. . . . The 'tenderfoot' who goes among them should

first double his life insurance and then be sure he is 'well-heeled.'"

Such disparate descriptions of the cowboy are the best proof that outsiders simply didn't see the whole picture. And yet, to be fair, the insiders didn't quite get the outsiders either. Like any group bound together and isolated by their work, cowboys all too frequently grew estranged from the "civilized" world, ceased to understand it, scorned its values and conventions—and eventually couldn't care less what it thought of them, either. In *A Cowman's Wife*, Mary Kidder Rak tells about ranch life in southwestern Arizona. She posed a basic question that likely occurred to many ranch women: "I cannot imagine that the clergyman believes that every man should be able to deliver a sermon, or that the hardware merchant expects everyone to know the price of nails. Then why should a cowman judge the rest of humanity upon the basis of a familiarity with the cattle industry? I find that my husband is by no means alone in doing so."

This insider-outsider gap has probably contributed to both the vilification and the idealization of the historic cowboy. Misunderstandings of his behavior, viewed superficially, were propagated early on in pulp fiction, novels, art, circuses, and rodeos, and were later on perpetuated and even further exaggerated by radio, film, and television. So many decades of so much inaccuracy make a lot of people think it's not really possible to know the *real* cowboy at all anymore. Believing Hollywood's version of the American cowboy, they think he popped up just after the Civil War, rode around for a couple of decades, and then disappeared into the dustbin of history.

The truth is that *real* cowboys still exist today. And even the cowboy of "the good ol' days" is not nearly

9

as distant as many people think. Under the right circumstances, Westerners in general, and cowboys in particular, are great storytellers. (Some of those stories might even be true!) Many cowboys and -girls wrote memoirs and autobiographies, kept diaries, corresponded vigorously, or were interviewed by others. Artists painted realistic Western scenes and journalists and travelers photographed frontier moments. Through these authentic cowboy voices and images, from both the past and present, the *truth* about the cowboy, his work, his life, and his world, can be discovered—and that's just what we intend to do here.

The real story of the cowboy both predates and antedates the brief golden age of trail drives and open-range ranching (from about 1867 to 1887), and this book tells and shows that exciting story in its entirety, from the cattleman's early roots to his modern incarnations. Throughout, we draw upon lots of true tales, in effect letting cowboys speak for themselves. Imagine having logged twenty miles trailing a herd of wild and ornery— the cowboy would say "ringy"—Longhorns. Now settle in beside a glowing campfire and listen to the adventures of cowboys from all over the West and from all decades of their history.

As you ride along with them, you'll probably be surprised at just how different cowboys were from one another, and might ask yourself, "What was it, then, that bound them all together?" Quite simply: a love of the work. As you read about the hardships of cowboy life, however, that answer just seems crazy, and you may well ask, "But what did they find so appealing about their rough, dangerous, thoroughly misunderstood jobs?"

One thing is certain: it wasn't the money. James Childers, born in Kentucky in 1857, began working in 1865 (that's eight years old!) on ranches in "No-Man's Land" (the Panhandle of western Oklahoma). As a "greener" (one who had not learned the work of a cowboy), Childers earned $25/month for his first year. With more experience, his wages eventually rose to $40/month. That wasn't much, but it was a relatively good wage for a cowhand. It could be much worse: In 1884, Georgia-born W. L. Rhodes began working at age twelve, rounding up cattle in Kaufman County, Texas. Over the next three years, his wages rose from $10/month to a "top hand's pay,

Opposite: *Modern-day cowboy, El Reno, Oklahoma, 2004.*

Above: *Unidentified boy in Western boots and hat. Photographed by Ralph R. Doubleday, circa 1945.*

which was $25.00 a month with chuck and all my riding string furnished [six to eight good mounts]."

Notice the pay. Notice the age. Cowboy work must have seemed exciting. In 1875, ten-year-old Henry Young even ran away from home to be a cowboy (and made an average wage at $25/month). But not all cowboys started work so young, and certainly cowboying wasn't all fun and adventure. So if it wasn't something in the nature of a boy or man that attracted him to the profession in the first place, there must have been something that cowboying developed in him that made him stay. Listening to cowboys talk about their intense love of their intensely difficult work, you'll start to see that the answer is a combination of both.

Jim Eike, a New Mexico rancher, believes that cowboys have to "like being cold and being hungry and wet and dirty and dusty and dry. It just takes

continued on page 14

He is slow of speech, but quick of hand, and keen and true of eye,

He is wise in the learning of nature's school—the open earth and sky;

His strength is the strength of an honest heart, he is free as the mountain's breadth;

He takes no fear of a living thing and makes a jest of death.

"The Rough Rider," by Richard Linthicum. 1900.[2]

Dodge City sign, designed by the Leadership Dodge Class of 1996, dedicated 1998.

Mabel Strickland.
World's Champion Cowgirl
Bell Photo
542.

Above: *Mabel Strickland, World's Champion Cowgirl. Bell Photo, circa 1930.*

Opposite: *Bronco busting, Bar Diamond range, circa 1909. Photographer Erwin E. Smith.*

a certain kind of man to be a cowboy." His wife Sharon added, "I think that cowboys have a special feeling for nature, an appreciation for life that is immediate. They see the babies, the calves, the renewal every spring of the grass and the wildflowers. I think it's just something about them that a lot of people don't have."

Cowboys may not have actually *liked* the hunger and the rough weather, but they certainly had to be able to tolerate it in good humor. In *Dakota Cowboy*, Ike Blasingame wrote of his life on the South Dakota range during the first decade of the twentieth century. He began working for the Matador Ranch after arriving in the state in 1904. "We put in long hours in the saddle," he recalled, "and made roundup after roundup. . . . We were pelted with rainstorms; hail pounded us a lot; wind beat the hills and dried the range. But, we had long, pleasant days, too, and the hours flew by. We were a well-fed crew, well mounted, and liked our work."[5] Perhaps an appreciation of the simple pleasures in life, the ability to look forward to better things to come, is what kept so many cowboys on the job.

continued on page 18

The bawl of a steer

To the cowboy's ear

Is music of sweetest strain;

And the yelping notes

Of the gray coyotes

To him are a glad refrain.

"The Cowboy's Life," Author unknown. 1908.[4]

Bunch of genuine, old-time cowboys and bronco busters at Denver, Colorado. Photographed by Solomon D. Butcher, 1905.

Above: *Ephraim Swain Finch branding cattle on the Milldale Ranch near Arnold, Custer County, Nebraska. Photographed by Solomon D. Butcher, circa 1900.*

Likewise, Ray Holmes, who worked on various ranches in northeastern Wyoming from the 1930s through the 1960s, most fondly recalls being outdoors, surrounded by the animals, with a sense of fulfillment at the work being done:"The best time of all to me, though, is in June when the grass is green, the cows are all scattered out, the calves are on the ground, and the branding is done. There's nothing nicer than to ride out on a good stout horse among a bunch of cows when they're all doing good, looking over the nice grass and knowing the cattle are all taken care of."

Such closeness to nature can instill an admiration and love of animals in any man, but cowboys *had to be* astute observers of nature and animals in order to succeed. Holmes himself noted that "one babysitter cow may be looking after three or four calves, whose mothers are off in the hills underneath the sagebrush or in the draws. I don't know how they decide which cow is to babysit, but that's what they do. The babysitter fends off would-be predators, such as coyotes, that might attack a lone calf."[5] Such shrewd per-

continued on page 23

Below: *William A. Shelbourn ranch on the Snake River, south of Valentine, Cherry County, Nebraska. Photographed by Solomon D. Butcher, circa 1900. [In 1995, Bob Bishop identified this photograph as: William Shelbourn on horseback, holding Henry; his wife Ida Mae (Wallingford) on the left, holding daughter Fan (Henry and Fan are twins); Florence and Joe Shelbourn are in the middle of the picture.]*

ception was a skill the cowboy needed literally every minute, sometimes even in order to save his life. Cowboying during the 1890s, W. H. Thomas slept "out under the stars with a slicker for a cover, my saddle blanket for a mattress, my boots under my neck and my saddle for a pillow." On cold nights, he continued, "I've woke up with sand rattlers and diamond backs too. They would crawl in under the blanket or slicker for the warmth. As long as you didn't hurt them, they wouldn't bite you."

While it would be difficult for a cowboy to succeed without these characteristics, even a miserable failure of a cowboy might find it hard to leave his job. Historian Tom Woods explains that people develop a sense of place

The smell of the rain-swept prairie

Blew up on us strong and sweet,

And all the music we needed

Was the ring of the unshod feet.

"Our Last Ride," by Rhonda Sivell. 1912.

Ned Dunlap, foreman on the Watson Ranch near Kearney, Nebraska. Photographed by Solomon D. Butcher, 1901. Dunlap had a degree in agriculture from the University of Nebraska and was a man of many talents. In this photograph, he is tricked out to participate in the Old Settler's Day Parade in Kearney in 1902. For that parade, Dunlap bobbed the tail off his horse and crammed it under his hat. He then affixed a horn to his head, pulled hooves up into his shirt sleeves, and marched as Kearney's only real Cow-Boy!

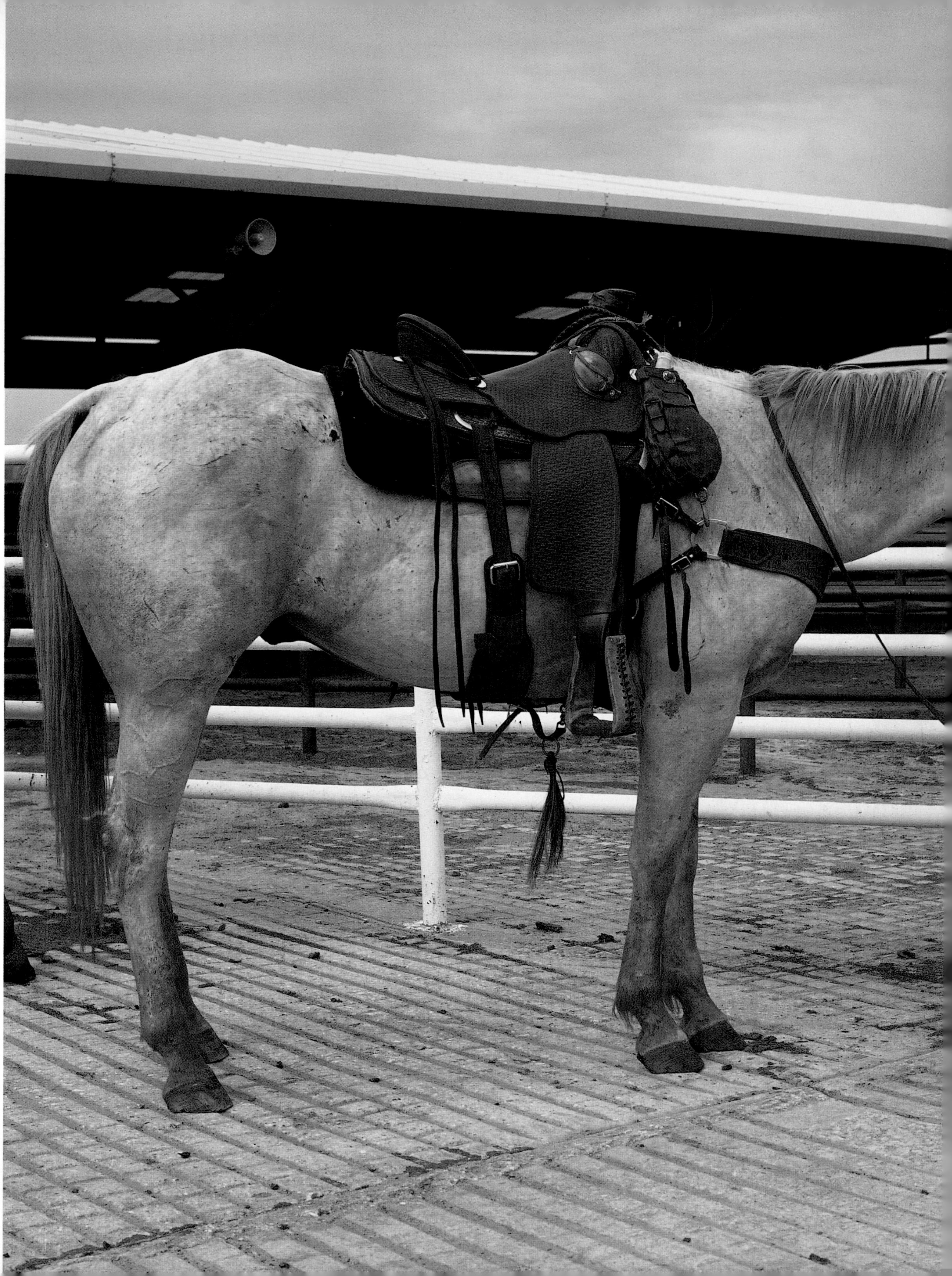

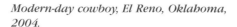

Modern-day cowboy, El Reno, Oklahoma, 2004.

through experience and knowledge of a particular area. A sense of place emerges through knowledge of the history, geography and geology of an area, its flora and fauna, the legends of a place, and a growing sense of the land and its history after living there for a time. In these days of chronic relocation, it might be hard for us to understand that, for cowboys and other ranchfolk, the Western landscape, its natural features, wild and domesticated animals, and other people combined to form a powerful magnet holding them to the land. To hear a cowboy tell it: "[T]o me the roar of a mountian stream mingled with the bells of a pack trane is grander musick than all the strings and brass bands in the world." So reads a 1923 letter from cowboy and Western artist Charles Marion Russell—who painted much better than he spelled!

To be sure, ranch work gave a whole new meaning to the phrase "worked a long day." Arkansas-born L. M. Cox ranched around Brownwood, Texas, beginning in the 1880s. "The cowboy's life as we know it was certainly lacking in the glamour which we see on our screens today," he said. "I have known cowboys to ride one hundred miles per day." Hands would eat breakfast before daylight, herd cattle until dark, and then it was not unusual to stand guard a good portion of the night. Most of us can't understand the eagerness to do a thing like that. Jim Eike must have been right: "It just takes a certain kind of man to be a cowboy."

Perhaps not unsurprisingly, these days the cowboy fares poorly in occupational surveys. In 2002, a survey of high school students ranked working as a cowboy 248th out of 250 occupations in desirability; only the fisherman and lumberjack ranked lower. Nevertheless, ranchers continue to raise cattle, and cowboys, with characteristic tenacity, courage, and loyalty, continue to "ride for the brand." Cowboys remain a breed apart, and their spirit, loyalty, and work ethic have stayed with them over the decades. While American history has shown few constants, cowboy life—lived, dramatized, imagined, or mythologized—may well be one of the few.

Even though hardly anybody wants to be a cowboy anymore, the cowboy image is as popular now as it ever was. According to Chuck Milner, working cowboy, singer, songwriter, and poet, the American cowboy retains his popularity because he stands for core values that many people identify with: "Independence, Individualism, and Integrity." In a world of increasing cynicism and moral relativism, these virtues resonate strongly with many. So cowboy life wasn't as glorious as all the Hollywood movies made it out to be, but it clearly was and still is at least worthy of nostalgia. That nostalgia, of cowboys writing, singing, speaking, joking, and otherwise telling their stories, is what distinguishes between the image and the reality—and it might just convince you that real cowboy life is even more fascinating than legend.

COWBOYS AROUND THE WORLD

While cowboys are certainly most often associated with the United States, famous, skillful equestrians have ridden in many other parts of the world. Ancient drawings suggest that nomads of the Cro-Magnon era, ten to twenty thousand years ago, may have fashioned halters or bridles to control horses.

Page 24: Canadian cowboy smoking pipe, with long Mexican-style taps over his stirrups, 1880s.

Page 25: Raul Moneta pets his Argentine criollo, *circa 1994–1995.*

Below: *A* gardian, *a cowboy in southern France, rides his white horse through a salt marsh in the Camargue.*

People known to us as Cimmerians likely rode horses on the Russian steppes about 7000 BCE, but we know little of their culture, because mounted Scythians from Turkestan invaded and conquered them about a millennium later. During the next two millennia, the latter became the world's first formidable equestrian culture, overrunning neighboring groups and spreading horsemanship onto the Iranian Plateau. Thereafter, equestrians flourished in the Middle East and China, and eventually carried their culture to western Europe.

Moving from prehistoric to historical times, we find records of the importance of horsemen in many regions of the world. Hebrew Scriptures describe some elements of livestock raising around 1960 BCE. In Genesis 13:7, we learn of an early range war: "And there was a strife between the herdmen of Abram's cattle and the herdmen of Lot's cattle." Horse and cattle trading apparently became well established among the Hebrews, as is evidenced by Genesis 47:17: "And they brought their cattle unto Joseph: and Joseph gave them bread in

exchange for horses, and for the flocks, and for the cattle of the herds, and for the asses: and he fed them with bread for all their cattle for that year." We also learn of the perils of equestrian life in Genesis 49:17. "Dan shall be a serpent by the way, an adder in the path, that biteth the horse heels, so that his rider shall fall backward."

When the Hyksos invaded Egypt about 1730 BCE, the horse provided a key element of their battle strategy. More than fifteen hundred years ago, Arabs of the Middle East became masters at breeding horses. Not only do Arabian mounts of today retain those ancient characteristics, today's Thoroughbred and American Saddle horse also show signs of their descent from early Arabian and Barb horses. Moors from north Africa brought this great equestrian subculture to Europe with their conquest of the Iberian peninsula early in the eighth century. Over time, the Moorish saddle and riding style, called in Spanish *a la jineta*, came to dominate Spanish horsemanship. The saddle provided a very comfortable ride and featured particularly short stirrups, which, when standing in them, gave the rider extra leverage to strike down at an enemy with a lance or sword.

Above: *A* gardian, *a cowboy in southern France, rides his white horse over dunes near the shore in Camargue.*

In the Camargue district of southern France, local legend has it that horses and cattle arrived from Asia well before humans. The Camargue, comprising some three hundred square miles, includes the Rhône river delta, with extensive marshes and lagoons—the perfect habitat for wild cattle and horses. The people here developed a unique breed of horse—small, strong, a bit wild, and with superb endurance. These animals may still be seen around the Vaccarès Lagoon in a regional park of some 203,000 acres. The *gardians* of Camargue proudly maintain their traditions, including an annual spring roundup and branding, known as the *ferrade*. Part roundup, part rodeo, and part fiesta, the event includes various riding and roping competitions, dances, and the branding of the wild herds (*manadas*). Their white horses amid black cattle and fierce fighting bulls make a dramatic, impressive picture. Elements of their dress and equipment resemble that of no other cowboy: Their black hats seem quite familiar to an American, but they wear wooden shoes, which are more appropriate to the wet environment, and still use tridents more often than lassos to handle bulls. A cultural organization called the *Nacioun Gardians* works to preserve the region's heritage.

continued on page 32

Below: *Argentinian* gauchos *cooking* asado *(roast) and drinking* mate *(tea), 1927.*

*Scène du campo –
Mettant l'anneau au bœuf.*

Above: *Argentinian* gauchos *putting a ring in a bull's nose, 1923.*

Left: *Argentinian* gauchos *staging a knife fight, circa 1900.*

And then the gaucho edged him in,
And pinned the plunging head;

They saddled him quick and gave him a lick,

And the breaker swung to the saddle slick,—

Ah, those were the times when the gaucho showed

The craft that is in him bred.

"Martín Fierro," by José Hernández (translated from Spanish into English by Walter Owen). 1872.

Huasos *(Chilean cowboys).*

Brazilian vaqueiros *lead a* boiada *(herd of cattle) from Paraguay to Cuiabá, the capital of the state of Mato Grosso in southwest Brazil, through the rough Mato Grosso countryside.*

In the 1490s, as Roman Catholic cavalry and other soldiers expelled the Moors from Spain after almost eight centuries of occupation, a noted Italian navigator, Christopher Columbus, carried horses, cattle, and the Moors' equestrian know-how on to the Americas. In the decades immediately after Columbus brought horses and cattle to the Caribbean, Spaniards began breeding them on the islands of Cuba and Hispañiola. Hernán Cortes introduced horses to Mexico in 1519, and the following year Gregorio Villalobos brought the first herd of cattle. As Spanish conquistadors fanned out across the North and South American continents, they spread their horses and cattle far and wide. As early as 1535, Jesuit missionaries raised livestock in the interior of South America, and by the 1540s wild livestock roamed the vast, fertile plains called *pampas* in Argentina, from where they pushed north into Uruguay.

Gauchos of Argentina and Uruguay began their long, colorful careers in the seventeenth century. Wild cattle vastly outnumbered domesticated animals at that time, so *gauchos* would hunt and kill wild cattle out on the pampas rather than herding domesticated animals. Wielding long lances tipped with crescent-shaped hocking blades, they slit the hamstrings of fleeing wild cattle—hundreds at a time—then returned to kill the downed animals with a formidable knife (*facón*) and stripped off and staked out the cowhide to dry. Argentina exported to Spain hundreds of thousands of such hides, along with tallow and other byproducts. By the eighteenth century *gauchos* produced and exported dried meat, which was fed to slaves in Brazil and the Caribbean. Throughout the region's tumultuous history, *gauchos*' unique military skills also qualified them for service as cavalrymen, and they participated in many conflicts.

On his epic journey around South America, naturalist Charles Darwin described Argentinian *gauchos* at a local tavern in 1832: "During the evening a great number of *Gauchos* came in to drink spirits and smoke cigars: their appearance is very striking; they are generally tall and handsome, but with a proud and dissolute expression of countenance. They frequently wear their moustaches and long black hair curling down their backs. With their brightly coloured garments, great spurs clanking about their heels, and knives stuck as daggers (and often so used) at their waists, they look a very different race of

Above: *Ben Fahey of Australia holds on to a bucking bronco during the Barretos Rodeo in Barretos, a city in the Brazilian state of Sao Paulo. Now billed as the largest cowboy festival in Latin America, the rodeo began in 1956 and is essentially a carnival done cowboy-style. The two-week event is held each year in August, and participants and fans travel from across Brazil and around the world to attend.*

Right: *Venezuelan* llanero *tailing a wild bull. Drawing by César Prieto, 1904.*

men from what might be expected from their name of *Gauchos*, or simple countrymen. Their politeness is excessive; they never drink their spirits without expecting you to taste it; but whilst making their exceedingly graceful bow, they seem quite as ready, if occasion offered, to cut your throat."

In the decades after Darwin's visit to the pampas, powerful landowners claimed the rich lands of Argentina and Uruguay. Gradually, *gauchos* who had hunted wild cattle went to work as ranch peons rounding up and branding their employers' domesticated cattle. Yet they retained their amazing skills of endurance riding, roping, and tossing *boleadoras*, three leather-covered stones connected by rawhide thongs. As with the American cowboy, technology eventually reduced the demand for *gauchos*, so that today we find *gauchos* performing for tourists about as often as they herd cattle. Writers in Argentina have found the *gaucho* an irresistible subject, and the great rider of the pampas has become a popular legend and national symbol almost as much as his northern counterpart. Most important among the works that established his dominance in Argentinian society are *Martín Fierro* (1872, 1879), a two-part epic poem by José Hernández, and *Don Segundo Sombra* (1926), by Ricardo Güiraldes.

Many other areas of the Americas also proved hospitable for grazing animals, and equestrian cultures developed in Chile (where the cowboy is called *huaso*), southern Bolivia, and the tropical plains of Colombia and Venezuela (where he is called *llanero*). Brazil features two types of cowboys: the *vaquiero* in the arid northeastern "hump," and the *gaúcho* in the southern state of Rio Grande do Sul. Mexico also gave rise to two equestrian traditions: the working cowboy (*vaquero*) and the landed aristocrat (*charro*).

Chile's *huaso* and southern Brazil's *gaúcho* might be thought of as the Argentinian *gaucho's* first cousins. They share many similarities in dress, vocabulary, and historical development. *Huasos* worked on ranches in the rich central valley of Chile, where, like the *gaucho*, they were mostly poor and dispossessed. As eventually happened to all ranch workers around the world, changing technology and market forces rendered many *huasos* unemployed in the late nineteenth century. Today, Chilean rodeo performers, with their bright red ponchos and oversized spurs, keep *huaso* tradition alive.

In 1715, Juan de Megalhaes established an *estancia*, or ranch, in Rio Grande do Sul, Brazil, marking the beginning of a conflict between the region's wild cattle hunters and the arriving ranchers who claimed exclusive rights to land, water, and animals. The same ranchers began producing jerked beef for the large slave populations in Brazil and Cuba. To serve this market, ranching in southern Brazil remained a primitive operation for much longer than in other South American countries, and new technologies, breeds, and practices arrived

there much later than in neighboring Uruguay or Argentina. Auguste Saint-Hilaire, a French traveler, recorded his impressions in the early 1820s: "The cattle are left completely to the laws of nature. They are not cared for in any way. They are not even given salt as the cattle in Minas [Gerais] are. They are almost wild." As with other cowboys in South America, the *gaúcho* became an important—if regional—figure in Brazil's literature and culture.

South American cowboys in Argentina, southern Brazil, Chile, and Uruguay worked in mostly fertile, hospitable plain regions. But the *llanero* of Colombia and Venezuela, from the colonial era through today, herds cattle in a much less inviting climate. The weather on the northern coast of South America alternates each six months between drenching, monsoon-like rains and searing heat and dust in the dry season. *Llaneros* have to move cattle upland from the flooded river plain during the wet season, then drive them back down to the lush lowlands after the rains subside... What a place to raise cattle!

Like the *gaucho*, the *llanero* always carries a large knife, in this case a machete. His roping style is unique, however, as Scottish writer Robert Bontine Cunningham Graham described: "He, of all wielders of the rawhide noose, alone secures it, not to the saddle, but to his horse's tail, fishing for, rather than lassoing, a steer, playing it like a salmon with a rope a hundred feet in length." As in Argentina, hides and dried beef constitute the main livestock exports from Colombia and Venezuela. Beef and coffee provide much of the *gauchos'* own sustenance, and a simple hammock serves as his bed. *Doña Bárbara* (1929), a novel by Venezuelan author Rómulo Gallegos, relates a compelling, memorable portrait of llanero life.

Above: *Rodeo clowns run to the aid of a bull-rider caught up in the ropes of a bucking bull at the Paniolo Heritage Rodeo, Molokai Ranch, Molokai, Hawaii.*

Opposite: Paniolo *in Kona, Hawaii drag cattle through the surf and tie them to the gunwales of longboats, which tow the animals to a larger ship.*

Cowboys have ridden the ranges of other continents, too. Around the turn of the nineteenth century, visiting sea captains gave the Hawaiian king gifts of livestock. The wild cattle multiplied to the point of threatening the island's agriculture and human population. Something had to be done. King Kamehameha III requested assistance from California, and, in 1832, a few Californian *vaqueros* sailed to Hawaii to help. They taught islanders how to handle cattle and horses, thus giving birth to Hawaii's cowboy, the *paniolo* (a term derived from *español*, or Spaniard). Despite lava flows, lack of ground water, and other obstacles, livestock ranching took root. Island cowboys gradually tamed the wild cattle, became expert horsemen, and developed their own *paniolo* culture, rooted in that of the *vaquero*. Ranching also spread from the "Big Island" of Hawaii to other islands. By the 1870s, Hawaiian ranches produced beef cattle and butter, which they shipped to Honolulu and then on to other markets. Immigrants soon joined native Hawaiians in working cattle, such that modern ranches employ cowboys of Irish, Portuguese, Japanese, Filipino, and other ancestry. Today, working ranches, historical societies in Kona and Waimea, rodeos, and trail rides preserve the *paniolo* heritage of Hawaii.

Australia's famed drovers have tamed horses and herded cattle and sheep for a century and a half, often aided by their skillful cattle dogs. As on most cattle frontiers around the world, cow*boys* predominated. In 1950, however, Edna Jessop, the fifth child of a drover family, became Australia's first female boss drover. She and her brother moved a herd of 1,550 animals some 1,400 miles after her father fell ill. The Australian Stockman's Hall of Fame and Outback Heritage Centre commemorates the history, culture, and lore of drovers, white and aboriginal, as well as other inhabitants of the outback. The center is located in Longreach, in central western Queensland.

Western Canada, and particularly British Columbia and Alberta, represents another cowboy culture. The many gold strikes in nineteenth-century western Canada each precipitated a livestock boom, as miners needed beef for food, as well as plenty of draft animals. The largest cattle boom in Canadian history occurred in Alberta and ran from the 1880s through about 1905. After open-range ranching in the United States collapsed in the mid–1880s, this Canadian livestock boom attracted many American cowboys, who migrated north to work on Alberta's ranches. The *Macloud Gazette* (November 30, 1886) recorded the impact of ranching on southern Alberta society: "The lasso and lariat, the broad-rimmed cowboy hat, the leather breeches, and imposing cartridge belts . . . are reproduced in this district in the same reckless

and extravagant fashion. The cowboy dialect rules supreme in the talk of the people. . . . The cowboy who can ride the fastest and 'round-up' the largest herd is the popular hero in this part of Alberta." In the early twentieth century, dry-land farming displaced many of the cattle herds in western Canada. Nonetheless, ranching remains a vital activity there even now, and the famed Calgary Stampede preserves the region's ranch and rodeo heritage.

In this quick ride around the world, someone's favorite cowboy has doubtless been left out. Russia's famous *kazaks*, or Cossacks, for example, functioned more as a military force than as cattle-herding cowboys, so they didn't make the cut. Because of his legendary status and importance as an international symbol, we'll spend most of the rest of this book exploring the life and times of the American cowboy. But many nations from all the corners of the earth have developed cowboy and equestrian cultures, and each one's history is about as unique and fascinating as the next. For that reason, I encourage you to find out all you can about as many as you can—maybe you'll be inspired to go out and ride with some.

Page 38: *A "jackaroo" or "ringer" (cowboy) musters (rounds up) cattle at a cattle station (ranch) in Australia's Northern Territory.*

Above (left): *John Ware, ex-slave, Canadian roper and rancher, his wife Mildred, and their two children.*

Above (right): *Woman at first Calgary Stampede, Alberta, Canada, 1912.*

Right: *Tom Three Persons, a Kainai (Blood) native and champion saddle bronco rider, at first Calgary Stampede, Alberta, Canada, 1912.*

COWBOY & RANCHING ROOTS

Like much else in American life, the cowboy's language, his tools, techniques, his favorite mount, the cattle he herded—even the cowboy himself—are all amalgams. In this case, Spanish origins laid a foundation that indigenous and later British components and influences would adjust to create the perfect mix for the American cowboy.

Page 40: *Longhorn skull and cowboy implements, Oklahoma City, 2004.*

Page 41: *Tony Esquival, a champion vaquero and star of Buffalo Bill's Wild West Show, poses on horseback in a dirt arena for the show at Ambrose Park in Brooklyn, New York. Photographed circa 1894.*

Above: *A Mexican vaquero poses over a horse lying on the ground while touring with Buffalo Bill's Wild West Show. Photographed between 1885 and 1900.*

The Spanish influences we see in the American West were brought by soldiers, missionaries, and settlers who fanned out across the frontiers of the Western hemisphere and often set up ranches. The American cowboy, however, typically inherited this culture indirectly, that is, through the Mexican vaquero who had learned his equestrian techniques and ranching skills from the Spanish conquistadors. In fact, this Spanish heritage is common to both the entire North and South American continents. We find that ranch hands from Tandil, Argentina and Abilene, Kansas to Alberta, Canada and Kona, Hawaii exhibited many commonalities.

Where there are variations from the pure Spanish tradition, we can usually see where they come from, and they are revealing and interesting in themselves. Each region's cowboys had contact with different native tribes, for example, and so each one learned slightly different ways of doing things. The Anglo cowboy, who learned from local natives as well as from the Mexican vaquero—who had also learned not just from Spaniards but different native tribes—really owes his ranching culture to many, many contributors. Writing in 1910, Michael J. Herron aptly summarized the cultural fusion that produced

Western American ranch life when he described the cattle frontier as a place "where the Anglo-Saxon and the Aztec met and mingled." Soon British immigrants and other Europeans would make their mark on the American cowboy as well.

All along, the unique landscape and climate of a region determined what modifications a cowboy himself had to make to that which he learned from other cowboys. For example, cowboys in Texas used shorter ropes than South American cowboys, because a long rope was easily tangled up in brush country. It is also thanks to the thorny brush that the Texas cowboy often sported leather leggings. Cowboys on colder northern ranges sometimes wore "woolies," chaps covered in angora or sheep wool for added warmth. In addition to natural surroundings, the level of a country's industrialization determined whether a cowboy made his own clothing, tools, equipment, and horse jewelry or simply purchased factory-made items. Of this specific landscape, particular mix of cultures, and unique combination of social and economic factors, the most recognizable American in the world was born—the cowboy.

Below: *A Longhorn grazes on prairie grass in the 40-acre Longhorn Park, located at the entrance to Dodge City Municipal Airport, Kansas, 2001.*

Christopher Columbus brought the first cattle to the Caribbean in 1493. Hernán Cortes and Gregorio Villalobos then brought cattle from Cuba to Mexico in the early 1520s, from whence they spread both north and south. Cattle, pigs, and goats provided a portable commissary for the conquistadors, and escaped, traded, and stolen livestock quickly became an important part of many indigenous cultures and economies. Horses and cattle found a variety of congenial environments throughout the Americas, and so herds of both proliferated not just in the American Midwest, but also on Argentina's vast, fertile pampas, in the tropical plains or *llanos* of Venezuela and Colombia, in Spanish California, on the island of Hawaii, and elsewhere.

Since America's many climates were so supportive of livestock, herders began handling cattle in many parts of the Americas. However, early horsemen did not work tamed cattle, but rather hunted and killed wild ones for their hides, tallow, and sundry byproducts. The rest of the carcass, including most of the meat, rotted on the plains and fed scavengers. A

Opposite: *Riding a Longhorn, Fort Worth Stockyards, Texas, 2001.*
Below: *Cowboy on horse. Photographed by Robert Runyon.*

Above: *Saddle Shop. Photographed by Carl Darr, 1984.*

cowboy in Latin America might kill an animal just to eat a single meal, perhaps the prized tongue. In some cases, ranchers dried meat into jerky and sold it to Brazilian and Caribbean plantation owners to feed their slaves.

The storied Longhorn has its roots in the Andalusian cattle (called *Retinto* or Spanish creole) brought by Columbus in the fifteenth century. Beginning in the 1820s, Anglo-American immigrants from the East brought English cattle westward, which interbred with the Andalusian cattle, resulting in the Longhorn we know today. Folklorist J. Frank Dobie estimated the genetic contributions to the Longhorn at 80% Spanish and 20% other, British-origin breeds. Most of this breeding occurred accidentally and at random, as cattle roamed freely and met upon the plains. Nevertheless, the Longhorn turned out to be quite a lucky mix: both Mexican and Anglo-American ranchers noticed that the crossbreed seemed particularly well adapted to the arid West, with good disease resistance, heat tolerance, stamina, longevity, and ease of calving, all of which were important to survival in harsh plains conditions.

There was a downside to that luck, though. The Longhorn could reach a weight of 1,800 pounds, and its horn span was considered average at four feet, but could reach lengths of up to nine feet. This enormous size and frightful horns made the Longhorn especially dangerous to handle. To top things off, he had an inherently irascible nature, and many were wild or semi-wild at best, living their entire lives isolated from humans until rounded up for the drive north. Cowboys (and their mounts) were particu-

Above: *Typical Western stock saddle. Ties held in place with silver conchos. A lariat hangs from front right side and an example of braided horsehair hangs from the saddlehorn. The relatively small saddlehorn shows that the rider did not dally rope.*

larly wary of the breed, and horror stories of cowboy-Longhorn run-ins were well known throughout the West. Dakota cowboy Ike Blasingame, for instance, once ran afoul of a Mexican Longhorn. He tightened the cinch on his horse, "Little Pete," and roped "a leggy dun-yellow longhorn around the horns. Before I knew what had happened, all three of us were down in one pile. I rolled out of the heap with a broken leg, a badly mashed ankle, deep bruises, and a general shaking up. The nearest doctor was at Evarts [South Dakota], 25 miles away."[6] In at least one case, however, those long horns spelled salvation for a fallen cowboy. As the *Cheyenne Daily Leader*

Quarter horse,
Oklahoma, 2004.

(Wyoming, August 2, 1882) reported, "Not long since a herder was knocked down by a wild steer and his face disfigured for life. His nose was torn completely from his face. That he was not killed was owing to the fact that the long horns, wide apart, touched the ground on either side of the poor fellow's head as he lay prostrate."[7]

Not until the late nineteenth century, with the advent of refrigeration, did beef become a major export from the Americas to Europe. At that point, wild cattle hunters in both North and South America were replaced by ranch hands herding domesticated cattle, and other European influences joined those of the Spanish (or Portuguese in Brazil) ranching pioneers. Even though their thick hides maintained export value, the old, tough, lean Longhorn cattle did not measure up to market requirements when chilled beef became the export of preference. Thus a variety of European cattle, notably Herefords and Angus, began to supplant earlier breeds. Stockmen recognized the increasing worth of their livestock, and branding and fencing became necessary to identify and control one's herds, a story explored later on.

Horses arrived in the New World along with the cattle and other livestock brought by Spanish conquistadors in the early sixteenth century. Thereafter, the horse played a key military and logistical role in Spanish warfare against the indigenous population of the Americas. The first breed introduced was the small, stocky "Spanish pony," which creative breeders in colonial Virginia and North Carolina crossed with English thoroughbreds during the eighteenth century to create a better cow horse. The resulting quarter horse, as it was called, showed great short-distance speed (hence the name), tremendous agility, and commendable "cow sense"—in other words, it was the ideal mount for working cattle.

As American pioneers moved westward through Tennessee, Kentucky, and into Texas and the rest of the American West, they brought their quarter horses with them. Soon the excellent cow horse had become crucial to herding and handling first wild and later domesticated cattle on the vast plains and ranches. W. L. Rhodes, who cowboyed in Texas during the 1880s, well explained the importance of his horse: "You see, a cutting hoss [horse] is as important to a cow poke as a hammer is to a carpenter. If your hoss is

continued on page 52

Pages 50–51: *Modern-day cowboy, El Reno, Oklahoma, 2004.*

Below: *Parade saddle, heavily silver mounted, floral tooling, ornamented with gold overlay, Texas-style skirt, wide swellfork, gold-capped horn, low cantle, long silver-mounted shield-style tapaderos. Includes breastcollar and bridle. Cantle plate engraved. Made by Herman H. Heiser, Denver, Colorado, circa 1950.*

trained right, and is a good hoss to start with, you can go into the herd, and cut the critter you want out of the herd, you just have the hoss push against it, or hit it with your lasso. Then your hoss will stay behind that critter 'til it gets out of the herd, and will chase it plum through the herd if necessary."

No less important than the horse itself was the saddle a cowboy needed to ride it. A cowboy could suffer no greater disgrace than if he were forced to "sell his saddle." Indeed, the saddle represented the cowboy's most important piece of equipment—and it had to fit just right. Different terrains and different cattle forced saddlemakers to innovate: the vaquero's technique of "dally roping" (wrapping the rope around the saddlehorn for leverage when lassoing an animal) necessitated the large horn found on the Mexican saddle. Cowboys riding in mountainous terrain might need a double-rig (a saddle with two girth straps to hold it in place). None of these functional differences would have meant anything at all, though, if a cowboy refused to be seen on a particular saddle. Hence, vaqueros and cowboys also indulged their sense of style and fashion, and silver conchos, leather straps, intricate tooling, and other affectations adorned more expensive saddles. Between functionality and decoration, a saddlemaker could create a virtually infinite variety of saddle styles, from the mundane working Western stock saddle on one extreme, to the Hollywood varieties (as seen in the Pasadena Tournament of Roses Parade) on the other.

The rope or lariat (from Spanish *la reata*) was the cowboy's key tool when herding.

Vaqueros braided their reatas, as long as one hundred feet, out of rawhide. During the late nineteenth century, ropes braided from Manila hemp (sisal) became popular. Cowboys called this new tool a "grass rope" and found them cheaper and stronger than rawhide lariats. During the twentieth century, nylon and propylene replaced hemp rope on many ranches. These synthetic materials became especially welcome in wet climates and where cowboys had to work animals around water.

James Childers aptly summed up the rope's importance: "The lariat is the key to a cowboy's success as a workman, and I determined to master the art. I was successful and at the end of my first year's work, I could place the loop where I desired quite accurately." While Anglo cowboys did sometimes become highly skilled ropers, many observers, including cattle buyer Joseph G. McCoy, expressed special admiration for the *vaquero's* superb skills. In 1868, McCoy watched two *vaqueros* chase a large buffalo: "In the twinkling of an eye their lariats were around his neck. . . . It was very exciting to witness the feat of lassoing one of those powerful monsters; to see how skillful those Spaniards could throw the lariat, and above all, how well trained were the horses."

Where did the cowboy get his equipment and tools? Well, as in the case of the reata, early *vaqueros* and cowboys made most of their own equipment themselves from the abundant leather available on any ranch. Soft horsehair provided the basis for other items, such as hackamores. Durability and practicality reigned as the most important qualities for riding gear, and so, for example, spurs were reduced in size as horses became tamer and more expensive. Gradually, more skilled and specialized artisans took over the manufacture of such items, as cowboys began to demand better, often customized gear. Silver decoration, frequently based on Spanish/Mexican motifs, adorned some such specialty equipment. By the late nineteenth century, however, cheap but highly durable machine-made equipment appeared out West from Eastern factories, and the expensive hand-tooled rawhide of specialized artisans gave way to less expensive production and materials. Today's riders have created a renewed market for handmade riding gear, thereby reviving the tradition of old-time leather-working.

There were a few things the cowboy rarely made, and his clothing, boots, hat, and gun (if he had one) were among them. Even these articles served a purpose in his work and had to be as functional as they were attractive. The *Democratic Leader* (January 11, 1885), of Cheyenne, Wyoming, left a portrait of cowboy dress at the height of the golden age of ranching and trail riding: "The

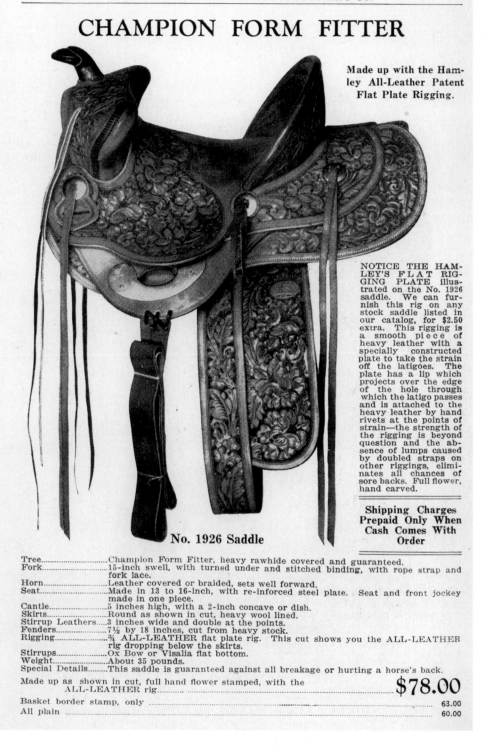

Opposite: *"Champions Ride Visalia Saddles." Visalia Stock Saddle Company, catalog no. 32, page 22. 1940.*

Above: *The Western Saddle Manufacturing Company, price list no. 42, page 10. 1932.*

Above: *"Yours truly, 'Jack' Elliott."*
Portrait of a man in cowboy clothes,
including woolies (chaps), a bandana,
felt hat, spurs, saddle, leather gauntlets,
and lariat.

sombrero is the cheapest and most comfortable hat. It is a shade to the eyes and protection to the skin, and although it costs from $7 to $15 to begin with, it lasts from four to six years, and can be cleaned like any other cloth garment. The flannel shirts are both warm and cool. There is no laundry for linen about the ranch. The corduroy trousers are most serviceable for riding horseback, as the English fox hunters long ago decided, and it is economy to wear the leather leggings in the mesquite underbrush, where cloth is but a poor armor. There is no affectation about the dress, considering all things."

Broad-brimmed hats and high-top boots were of course the most identifiable and functional elements of the cowboy's dress. In addition to shading the eyes and protecting the skin, the hat served many, many other purposes. Jack Rollinson, in his description of the Wyoming cowboy's dress during the 1890s, listed just a few: "All wore Stetson hats of the high-crowned pattern— most of which looked like they had seen plenty of service, as indeed they had, for those hats had fanned many an ember into flame for a fire; had served to dip into a creek or water hole to drink from; had been used to spook a horse alongside the head, or to slap him down the rump."

The cowboy boot's trademark narrow, pointed toe permitted the cowboy to slip his foot quickly and accurately into the stirrup. The high heel hugged the stirrup and kept the cowboy's foot from sliding through. Cowboys willingly paid $12 to $20 a pair for "custom-mades" that were fitted to the individual's foot. Generally, they favored boots a foot or more high to protect the lower leg from brush and thorns and to keep dirt out, though height and style were also subject to fashion trends. During the 1870s, for example, cowboys favored taller styles, from 14 to 17 inches high. Just after the Civil War, a particular style of boot called the "Coffeyville boot" (of Kansas) gained popularity for its large mule-ear bootstraps, which aided a man when pulling them on. Still, there was only one type of boot that became a Western synonym for quality boots—the Stetson of footwear, so to speak: "Big Daddy Joe" Justin and family of Spanish Fort, Texas, are credited in "bootlore" (or "footlore") as the creators of the first ever Anglo-made cowboy boots, and the name "Justins" is still used as a substitute for "boots" in cowboy lingo today.

What came between head and foot was just as important, and the cowboy took care to make sure his pants, shirt, leggings, and "accessories" both suited his style and would hold up to wear for a good long time. In 1875, when Henry Young got work on Bill Adair's CA Bar Ranch near Colorado City, Texas, the rancher bought the youngster

JESS WILLARD HIMSELF The Cowboy Champion with 101 Ranch Wild West

Above: *"Jess Willard Himself: The Cowboy Champion with 101 Ranch Wild West." Unknown photographer, circa 1915.*

Right: *Advertising card, Stetson Hats, Hirshfeld & Anderson, Austin, Texas, circa 1935.*

"California pants, the kind of pants all cowhands wore those days in that section. The pants were made from heavy woolen plaid cloth. He had the pants half-soled, as we called it. That was to reinforce the seat with soft leather so they would stand the saddle wear." Young also got a bandana and a silk handkerchief that he wore as a necktie, which served his needs as well as his vanity. In the absence of women out on the frontier, silk became a common material for such garments, since it required no ironing and could be easily laundered by bachelors.

As some of the original rugged individualists, cowboys did not all dress alike—at least not across state lines. While fashion consciousness tended to create trends among cowboys from the same region, climate and functionality demanded cowboy clothing and equipment be adapted to circumstances. Jack Rollinson, who described the many uses of the cowboy hat earlier, said of the same Wyoming cow hands: "They were quite uniformly dressed, and the majority of them wore tight-waisted blue denim Levi Strauses, with hickory shirts or some light cotton shirt. They also wore a black silk bandanna bout their throats. . . . Some of the men wore heavy leather belts and some went without a belt, while others wore suspenders. Many of the riders wore vests,

MILES CITY SADDLERY CO. MILES CITY, MONT.

Makers of the Original Coggshall Saddles

Stetson's Cowboy and Ranchmen's Hats

Carlsbad.   Gray or Brown.   Price - - - - - - - $12.00
             3X Beaver quality.   Price - - - - - - 20.00
             Tobacco Brown (made to order only) 3X Quality   20.00

Carlsbad.   White, Black or Brown Velour.   Price - - $20.00

"Powder River."   White, Black or Brown Velour.   Price $16.50
             Mailing weight 2 lbs.
             211

Above: *Stetson's Cowboy and Ranchmen's Hats, Miles City Saddlery Company, catalog no. 27, page 211. Circa 1905.*

for a vest was most handy, in that it had pockets for tobacco, matches, and other nicknacks."[8] To the northeast, however, in South Dakota, cowboy and rancher Ed Lemmon insisted that ranch hands there did not wear blue jeans made by Levi Strauss: "I never saw northern cowpunchers or cowmen wear overalls or Levis. I worked with range cattle from 1870 to 1923, and I never wore overalls until I got my first flivver, about 1907, and then I wore bib overalls. No, the only cowhands I ever saw in overalls were a few who came up the trail from Texas."[9] It made good sense, too: cowboys in hotter climates wore denim for the cloth's durability and ability to "breathe," which would not have suited cowboys in colder climates, who wore wool pants instead.

These days, cowboy dress and jewelry have become so popular in certain areas of the country that many people find it hard to distinguish between the real ranch hands and the merely trendy. In addition to cowboys and rodeo and other performers, many Westerners strive to preserve pieces of traditional cowboy culture as a legitimate art form. Handmade boots, saddles, hats, and "horse jewelry" have experienced a renaissance. Riders themselves now seek out quality, handmade saddles, bridles, and other gear, as well as custom-made spurs, belt buckles, and other specialty items to wear. Given this spirited resurgence in all things Western, is it even possible to spot a real working cowboy today? Douglas E. Johnson, of the TO Ranch, outside Raton, New Mexico, offered this advice: "When you see a sure-enough cowboy walk down the street, he's got a little swagger to his walk and his hat don't look near as pretty as some of them that just walked out of the store. You can just spot a riding hand pretty quick."

One of the myths about cowboys is that they rode around armed to the teeth. In fact, many ranchers were very aware of the inherent dangers of so much firepower and forbade sidearms on the range. Instead, cowboys carried a carbine in a leather saddle-mounted scabbard. Think of it: What working man

R.T. FRAZIER'S SADDLERY PUEBLO COLO.

CHAPAREJOS

No. 4206   **Price $28.75**

Angora fur, black, white or gold, with spots of contrasting color; wide flap leather lined; leg linen lined, snaps and rings; hand carved belt. Give length of inseam of pants when ordering.

Postage, 75c

No. 4207   **Price $25.50**

California oil kip leather; yellow or brown, wide flap; buckskin sewed; studded with German silver or brass spots and conchas. This is a very good chap and will give comfort.

Give length of inseam of pants when ordering.

Postage, 50c

No. 4208   **Price $23.50**

Angora fur, black, white or old gold; fringe at sides. The fur linen lined, buckskin sewed; backs made of buckskin tanned calfskin. The above cut shows the low shape belt. Give length of inseam of pants when ordering.

Postage, 75c

Above: Chaparejos, R.T. Frazier's Saddlery, Pueblo, Colorado, catalog no. 31, page 71. Circa 1931.

would want several pounds of leather and metal strapped around his waist during a long, arduous day on the range anyway? Despite this reality, we see in a statement from the *Las Vegas Optic* (New Mexico, June 28, 1881) a grim but common picture of the cowboy: "It is possible that there is not a wilder or more lawless set of men in any country that pretends to be civilized than the gangs of semi-nomads that live in some of our frontier States and Territories and are referred to in our dispatches as 'the cowboys'. . . . They roam about in sparsely settled villages with revolvers, pistols and knives in their belts, attacking every peaceable citizen met with."

The other half of this "shoot-'em-up" myth is that all cowboys were expert marksmen. Actually, few cowpokes matched the viciousness and marksmanship of the storied gunmen of the Old West, and so it is no surprise that the historical record is filled with accidents, often self-inflicted, as opposed to willful shootings. Dakota cattleman Ed Lemmon recalled a boy's death in 1906, during a train ride from Chicago to Kansas City. "It turned out that the boy had stuck the gun under his pillow the night before, the way he'd read all westerners did it, and the porter, when pulling the blankets off the berth to make it up, had knocked the gun off." It dropped to the floor, fired, and shot the youth through the abdomen.[10] Similarly, Ed Lemmon related the unhappy history of a pearl-handled Colt .45 that had belonged to one of his friends who had been killed in a gunfight. A cowboy named Oscar purchased the weapon, and "while flourishing the gun in Sidney [Nebraska], Oscar, who was somewhat lushed up [drunk], accidentally shot it off and killed himself. That seemed to be an unlucky gun."[11]

In all truth, gunplay and gun-related accidents did figure in the early demise of many cowhands, but the fatalities resulting from violence have been heavily exaggerated. Most cowboys, in fact, left a chamber of their six-shooter empty, as did Harry Buffington Cody: "The reason I only filled five was because I wanted to keep one chamber empty, fearing that I might have an accident." None other than famous marshal and gunman Wild Bill Hickok almost shot himself when his sidearm slipped from his holster and discharged on the floor. The very reality that all cowboys were *not* sharpshooters (or always sober, or always smart) was all the more reason *not* to run around armed to the teeth, and both cowhands and their employers took this fact very seriously.

How about the cowboy himself? Where did he come from? What did he look like? We've seen that English immigrants to the West brought new breeds of cattle and horses with them. Indeed, the majority of American cowboys were

Above: *The Justin Boot Company, N. Porter Saddle & Harness Company, catalog no. 64, page 45.*

Above: *"Woolies," chaps covered in fur or, more commonly, angora or sheep's wool. Such extra protection from cold was sometimes needed by cowboys on northern ranges.*

Opposite: *"Cowboy." Portrait of a man in cowboy clothes, including woolies (chaps), a bandana, felt hat, spurs, and lariat.*

of white European descent, just like the majority of American society in general. However, a very significant minority of working hands on the ranch and on cattle drives did not look like most peoples' idea of the prototypical cowboy. George W. Saunders, co-founder and president of the Old Time Trail Drivers Association (1915), estimated that from 1868 to 1895 about 35,000 men went up the trail, of whom approximately one-third were *vaqueros* and blacks.[12] Thus, like the horses, cattle, and ranch culture, cowboys themselves represented an amalgam of many different ethnicities and backgrounds.

The *vaquero*, or Mexican cowboy, sometimes comprised the majority of a ranch, sometimes a small minority, but wherever he was, he was significant regardless of numbers. He had "gotten here first," so to speak, and, as explored throughout this book, his many, many years of ranching and herding experience in the New World invested him with much to offer the European newcomers. By the time the Anglo cowboy arrived, the *vaquero* had had cowboying "in his blood" already for generations, and his white employers and fellow cowhands could tell it.

The historical record is full of Anglo cowboys' observations and admiration of the *vaquero* and his skills. Writing for *Harper's Monthly* in March 1894, Frederic Remington described his first look at Mexican *vaqueros*: "With their jingling spurs, their flapping ropes, and buckskin strings, and with their gay serapes tied behind their saddles, they were as impressive a cavalcade of desert-scamperers as it has been my fortune to see." Just listen to a cowboy talk, and you will quickly appreciate the extent of the *vaquero's*

N° 6 "COW BOY"

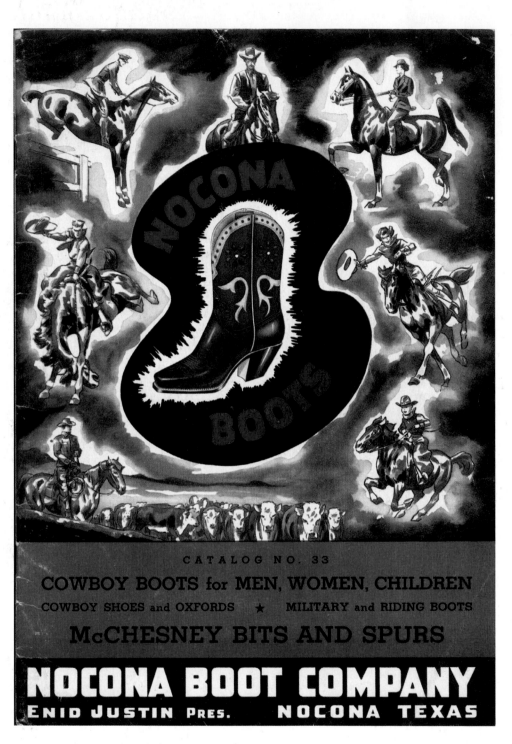

CATALOG NO. 33

COWBOY BOOTS for MEN, WOMEN, CHILDREN

COWBOY SHOES and OXFORDS ★ MILITARY and RIDING BOOTS

McCHESNEY BITS AND SPURS

NOCONA BOOT COMPANY

ENID JUSTIN PRES.   NOCONA TEXAS

Above: *Nocona Boots, Nocona Boot Company, catalog no. 33, front cover.*

Opposite: *Pedro "Joe" Esquivel, a champion* vaquero *and star of Buffalo Bill's Wild West Show, poses on horseback in a dirt arena for the show at Ambrose Park in Brooklyn, New York. He wears leather chaps and a cowboy hat and has a scarf tied around his neck. A landscape scene is painted on the backdrop. Photographed circa 1894.*

influence. He will show you his taps ("*tapaderas,*" stirrup coverings), chaps ("*chaparreras,*" leather leg-coverings), and McCarty (from "*mecate,*" fine, horsehair rope). If you gain his confidence, he might tell you about the unfortunate Saturday night that he spent in the hoosegow (from "*juzgado,*" or jail). Linguist Robert N. Smead has compiled an entire book of Western and ranching terms derived from Spanish sources, called *Vocabulario Vaquero (Cowboy Talk).*

While ranchers west of the Nueces River most often employed *vaqueros,* Texas ranches east of the Trinity River often had all-black crews. As one traveled north, the number of both Hispanic and black cowboys decreased, just as they did in the general population. (In 1870, for instance, Montana censuses counted only 183 black residents; in 1880, 346.) Black slaves had tended cattle, usually on foot, in the colonial Old South. Black jockeys, trainers,

and grooms handled the expensive quarter horses raised and raced by the Southern gentry. As Steven F. Austin and others brought Anglo immigrants to Mexican colonies in Texas, slave owners brought their slaves with them. By 1845, Texas had an estimated 100,000 whites and 35,000 slaves; by 1861, 430,000 whites and 182,000 slaves.

While slavery still existed, some odd discrimination occurred. Because of their value as property, slaves were sometimes treated better than (white) hired hands. Abel "Shanghai" Pierce tamed horses in Texas in 1853, assisted by several slaves. Pierce's superior ordered him to break the most dangerous

mounts, because the slave owner did not want to risk injuring slaves "worth a thousand dollars a piece." The boss considered Pierce—at just a few dollars a day—expendable.

Conditions worsened for Southern blacks when Reconstruction ended in 1877. As freed blacks sought better opportunities than available in the "redeemed" Old South, the number of African-Americans in the West swelled. In less than two years, from late 1877 through 1879, tens of thousands of ex-slaves migrated to Kansas. These were just a handful of the so-called "exodusters," as these African-American migrants called themselves,

continued on page 70

Above: *"Black men on horses." Group portrait of black men on horseback. Identified as Amos Maytubby (Choctaw), Deputy Marshal Zek Miller, Neely Factor, Bob L. Fortune.*

67

For if the Lord had meant us all

to be alike and the same rules to keep,

He would have bonded us all together

just like a flock of sheep.

"Be Yourself," by Georgie Sicking. 2001.

"Black cowboy and his horse." A black man poses with a saddled horse. Costume includes chaps and a bandana. Photographed between 1890 and 1920.

Left: Jicarilla *cowboy. Photographed by Edward S. Curtis, circa 1905.*

Opposite: *Studio portrait of Ben Pickett, brother or cousin of the famous bulldogger Bill Pickett, here misidentified as his famous relative. He holds a rope and wears cowboy boots, a vest, and wide-brimmed hat. He poses near a fur pelt on a pedestal. The inscription on the photograph reads: "Bill Pickett, Famous Negro Cowboy. First man bullogger [bulldogger] also used his teeth bull dogging instead of hands on horns method used by cowboys today." Photographed by Ralph R. Doubleday, between 1910 and 1930.*

drawing a parallel bet-ween the biblical story of the exodus of the Jews from slavery and oppression in Egypt and their own situation: escaping slavery in the South to reach "the promised land" in the West. Unfortunately, they usually found only bleak prospects, a harsh climate, and barren land, and in the end, only an estimated one -third stayed in the West. One African-American, an ex-Virginian slave named John Ware, actually became a well-known, successful rancher in Alberta, Canada, but his story is a rare exception that proves the rule of little upward mobility for blacks in the West.

Native Americans of the Great Plains and Southwest embraced the arrival of the horse early on, but always preferred buffalo to cattle. By the mid-eighteenth century, equestrian pursuits had transformed the economies, culture, and religion of many native groups in the West. However, their golden age of buffalo hunting ended in the 1870s when white migration, fueled by railroad access, overran their lands and hunted bison nearly to extinction. Looking for a new means of survival, some Native Americans turned to ranching, often on or near reservations.

Bill Pickett, Famous Negro Cowboy

First man bulldogger also used his teeth bull dogging instead of hands on horns method used by cowboys today

"Ute with firearms." Standing portrait of two unidentified Native American (Ute) cowboys. One holds a rifle and a horse by a rope; the other holds a pistol. Photographed between 1900 and 1930.

Horses retained their importance as a measure of status and wealth for many groups, including the Apache, Blackfeet, Crow, Hidatsa, Navajo, and Northern Cheyenne. Most groups preferred to raise horses on their ranches, but some Indians also raised cattle or worked as cowboys for other ranchers. Sam Yellow Robe, for example, a Rosebud Sioux born in 1890, worked on a number of Dakota ranches. Sam White Horse, born in 1897, worked his first roundup at age fifteen. Many reservations leased lands to white ranchers, and Indians provided much of the manpower. South Dakota, New Mexico, Arizona, and Oklahoma, with their larger Indian populations, had the most Indian cowboys.

Indian cowboys, just like other minority cowboys, were as much a part of cowboy life as any Anglo cowboy. In 1903, Laura Iversen Abrahamson worked at a restaurant in Fort Pierre, South Dakota, during a 4th of July picnic and specifically recalled the mix of celebrants: "People came from everywhere—ranchers, cowboys, Indians—we fed over five hundred people here in this place alone, and we were just two waiters."[13] Native Americans, like blacks and vaqueros, also competed in rodeos, exhibiting skills in a wide range of events. One of the best-known Indian rodeo performers was George Defender, who was born on the Standing Rock (Lakota) reservation in 1897 and became a highly skilled cowboy and rodeo bronco rider. Since World War II, the six-day "Crow Fair," independently organized by the Crow tribe, has attracted tens of thousands of people each year. Held in South Dakota each third week of August, the fair includes horse and foot races, rodeo, dancing, and other cultural events. Other native cultures enjoy similar gatherings on a smaller scale. As with other cowboys, the number of Native American ranch hands has diminished in recent years, but a small group does remain dedicated to working on horseback.

Despite their importance, most Indian, Hispanic, and black cowboys faced social and economic discrimination throughout the West, as they did elsewhere in the country. Whites routinely referred to Mexicans or Mexican-Americans as "greasers" and to blacks as "niggers." On Anglo ranches, discrim-

BUCK TAYLOR.
King of the Cow Boys.—*Buffalo Bill's Wild West.*

W. Wilson   PHOTOGRAPHER

ination usually took the form of lower pay for the same work. Prevailing attitudes also kept non-white cowboys from positions of authority, as many cowboys born in the South carried the racial prejudices of their time and would not abide taking orders from anyone non-white, no matter how skilled. Jim Perry, an African-American cowboy, worked for twenty years on the huge XIT ranch in Texas, which had seven divisions or ranges. "If it weren't for my damned old black face, I'd have been boss of one of these divisions long ago," he lamented. Instead he ended his days as ranch cook.

Women's presence in the West was significant and crucial, but there were nowhere near as many women as men, both on the ranch and on the trail, and so women seemed a great rarity to the cowboy. Women's proper roles in such a masculine environment were often a matter of controversy and were by no means consistent across class lines or static in the face of changing historical circumstances. In the chapters to come, we will see many examples of exceptional women, as well as "regular" women who performed more traditional women's work both on ranch and trail.

One of the most prominent women of the Old West was Elizabeth Ellen "Lizzie" Johnson. Born in Missouri in 1840, she registered her own cattle brand

COPYRIGHT 1909 BY
GEO. B. CORNISH,
ARKANSAS CITY, KANS.

THE BELLE OF THE RANCH.

Above: *"The Belle of the Ranch," George B. Cornish. Arkansas City, Kansas, 1909.*

Opposite: *Annie Oakley, wearing hat and two medals, holding rifle in both hands, one foot propped on edge of teepee. Full-length studio portrait with painted backdrop. Photographed by David F. Barry between 1897 and 1926.*

in Texas in 1871 and hired cowboys to gather mavericks for her herd. She made good money over the next several years, shipping her Texas cattle north. She also invested in real estate and showed considerable business sense, retaining control of her interests after marriage by means of a prenuptial agreement. In 1886 and several times thereafter, she hitched up a buggy and helped drive her own herds from San Antonio to Abilene. She sold the cattle at a good profit: indeed, at her death in 1924, she had amassed an estate valued at a quarter of a million dollars.

Even once the cattle, horses, tools, equipment, and all the varieties of cowboys and girls had converged upon the plains, ranching and cattle driving didn't just take off as a result of some perfect mix. The golden age of cowboying that popularized the whole Western scene to begin with was the result of societal, economic, and political factors as well. American expansion during the mid- and late nineteenth century shifted the country's attention west, and cowboys just happened to find themselves right in the middle of the new national stage.

The government, for one, played a major role in facilitating the expansion of Western ranching. During the 1870s, the US Cavalry pacified or removed Plains Indians, the last major threat to ranching. Hunters then destroyed the bison, thus removing the major grazing competitor to cattle. The government also paid ranchers for beef and livestock to supply Indian reservations and military forts, generating considerable demand.

In addition to government action, larger economic forces spurred a series of livestock booms. The Gadsden Purchase of 1853 added a vital trade

route in the Southwest and stimulated regional growth for Hispanics and Anglos. Gold rushes in Colorado in 1859 and Arizona in 1862 created demand for livestock. The expansion of railroads throughout the West generated other boomlets. Ranchers, attentive to any market demand, drove their cattle wherever the market dictated strong returns.

After the Civil War, when Texan soldiers returned home to an overabundance of cattle that rendered them worthless there, the great trail drives were kicked off to bring them to more profitable markets. These drives populated most of the Great Plains with cattle by the late 1870s, and this dispersion ushered in the great era of open-range ranching, when cattle ranged widely over the plains. Numbers grew quickly: In 1870, about 17 million beef cattle grazed in the United States. That figure jumped to 35 million by 1900, and 47 million by 1920. Western and Midwestern states held most of those cattle. Texas retained the top spot throughout the period, with 6.4 million beef cattle in 1900. Another 2.9 million cattle grazed in Kansas, 2.7 million in Iowa, and 1.9 million in Nebraska.

In 2001, raising cattle generated annual revenues of more than $40 billion. The same states that topped the cattle-raising charts a century ago continue to lead: Texas

is still at the top of total U.S. production with 16.8%; Nebraska, 12.5%; Kansas, 12.2%; Colorado, 6.4%; and Oklahoma, 4.6%. But come on, those are just boring old numbers! *How* those numbers rose as high as they are, on the other hand, is a long, fascinating tale. How the cattle got to market, who herded them, what hazards they faced along the way… this is the story of the growth of ranching and the rise (and fall) of the American cowboy. It is the transition from the Civil War to the golden age of cowboying to the modern, hi-tech ranch. And it's what we'll explore in the chapters to come—so saddle up!

Opposite: *"The Cow Boy." Photographed by J. C. H. Grabill in Sturgis, Dakota Territory, circa 1888.*

ON THE RANCH

Spanish colonists early established ranches and missions in Florida, Texas, California, and the Southwest, in some cases going back to the sixteenth and seventeenth centuries. As the predecessors of the ranches of the American West that began to flourish only after the Civil War, the Spanish and Mexican way of doing things influenced the American rancher in everything from clothing and cuisine to branding techniques and ranch organization. Immigrating Europeans did their part, as well, to shape the American ranch and the life of the cowboy into what we know and love today.

Page 80: *"Buffalo Vernon Bulldogging Steer." Photographed during the Cheyenne Frontier Days rodeo event, circa 1910.*

Page 81: *Charley Meeks, cowboy. Photographed by Solomon D. Butcher, 1886.*

Above: *Wyoming ranch, 2002.*

The Anglo rancher learned a lot from watching his vaquero workers do their jobs, but he also altered and developed much of what he borrowed. Plain old American ingenuity dictated that the best of all available ideas be combined to achieve the best result, and that meant adopting whatever tools and techniques best suited the American cowboy's circumstances. Hence, over the course of time, everything from the cross-breeding of cattle and horses to technology and the changing social roles of women have changed the face of the Western ranch drastically—so much, some old-fashioned cowboys would say, that it ain't even really cowboying anymore. In this chapter, we'll explore the golden age of ranching that we associate today with the great and glorious trail rides and roundups of yesteryear, the factors that brought that proud era to an end, and how Western life has gone on in the meantime.

In the mid- to late nineteenth century, ranches varied in size from a few hundred acres, with cattle in the dozens, to hundreds of thousands of acres, with herds in the tens of thousands. On smaller ranches, family members both young and old, male and female, usually handled all the chores; only during roundups would the ranch hire extra hands. At the opposite extreme, by the late nineteenth century Richard King's South Texas ranch included 1.27 million acres. His work force of 300 vaqueros tended 65,000 cattle and 10,000 horses. John Chisum's "Rancho Grande" straddled the

Interior of an old-time ranch, Powder River, Montana.
Photographed by L.A. Huffman.

borders of west Texas and eastern New Mexico. In a single season, his hands branded 18,000 calves. In 1886, the Swan Land and Cattle Company, Wyoming's largest ranching concern, owned 123,500 head of cattle grazing on 579,000 acres of land. These large ranches enjoyed large profits, until multiple disasters hit in the mid-1880s.

As Richard King's ranch shows, many of the workers on Western ranches were of Spanish or Mexican origin, and they brought with them their centuries of ranching experience in the New World. Many ranching techniques were learned or adapted from them, but the art of horse taming, developed over centuries in both Europe and the New World, is one of the most interesting and well-documented examples. In an age of plentiful horses, Mexican vaqueros took a direct, often brutal approach. In his *Guide to Texas Emigrants*, David Woodman, Jr. recounted the method he saw used by vaqueros in the region during the 1830s: "[B]y starving, preventing them from taking any repose, and continually keeping them moving, they make them gentle by degrees, and finally break them to submit to the saddle and bridle." In his cowboy memoir, Ross Santee described his experience with a very similar technique, evidence of the Anglo cowboy's indebtedness to his vaquero predecessor: "Each bronc was roped, an' after he choked down, a hackamore was put on his head. Then he was tied outside with a long rope, so's he could move around a lot."

There were, of course, other techniques as well. Skilled photographer L. A. Huffman described a bronc tamer at work in 1907. He used "just a plain, ordinary, single-rigged cow-saddle, bridle, and lariat, spurs, quirt, and some short pieces of grass rope for the cross-hobbling." Once snubbed and hobbled, the horse felt the bulk of a forty-pound saddle for the first time. The rider often twisted the horse's ear to distract him as he mounted the animal for the first time, then repeated bucking sessions eventually brought the horse under the rider's dominion. Savvy "peelers" even invented their own special techniques, often making ingenious use of the local terrain. Colorado cowboy William Henry Sears described a trick he used during the 1870s: "Always we took the wild horses to a large sand bar opposite old Fort Wise, and there these bronchos were broken. It did not take long for they were soon worn out from bucking in the deep sand."

Contrary to popular myth, not all cowboys could ride any horse alive. In fact, riding skills, just like roping and other abilities, varied widely. Only a handful of cowboys had the skill and grit to be bronco busters, but that special talent and horse sense earned him the esteem of his peers … and higher wages. A top hand who could tame wild horses represented the elite of cowboy ranks. Tom J. Snow, born in late 1863 in Cleburne County, Alabama, became a good rider as a teenager and soon joined that elite. "I was in demand as a horse wrangler," he noted. "I devoted five years to the business of breaking the wild critters and received $5.00 a head for the work." About 1870, young Harry Buffington Cody (called Buffalo Cody by his friends, because he once rode in Buffalo Bill's Wild West show) had reveled at earning $10 a month driving cattle up the trail from Texas to Kansas. A little later he earned $20 a month plus food working on Texas ranches. He then moved west to the Briscoe spread just below Uvalde, Texas, where he worked for four months, taming horses for "$30.00 a month and chuck." It didn't take Cody long to wise up and quit. "I realized that it was really worth a $100,000 a month and chuck because of the danger in busting wild hosses."

Below: *Two men on bucking broncos. Photographed by W. D. Harper, circa 1904.*

Lee Warren with bucking horse:
Saddling a bronco, first pull at latigo.

Giving the bronco a slicker lesson.

Giving the bronco a slicker lesson (continued).

Mounting the bronco, with the ear twist.

All photographed by L.A. Huffman, September 1904.

J. C. H. Grabill, Photographer,
STURGIS, DAKOTA TER.

Above: *Roping and changing scene on Cheyenne River. Photographed by John C. H. Grabill between 1887 and 1892.*

Opposite: *Unruly Butcher Bob at the Cheyenne Frontier Days rodeo event, circa 1910.*

Owing to those dangers, most cowboys who "snapped broncs" didn't enjoy long careers. Cody described one ride with a particularly tough horse. It "bucked all over the place 'til the blood ran from my nose and both my legs were plum raw from having the skin scraped off, trying to hold on." Ranch owners and foremen were not always so sensitive to the dangers, either, as in the experience of Oklahoma cowboy Raisins Rhoads. A bronc buster at the Chapman-Barnard Ranch in the 1940s, Rhoads was once ordered by the ranch foreman, Ben Johnson, Sr., to break some horses in a very rocky corral. "Ben," asked Rhoads, "what about all them rocks? He said when I turn this son-of-a-bitch loose, you're gonna try and ride him. You're not gonna want to fall down there on them rocks." Another Oklahoma cowboy, Dink Talley, had no regrets at leaving bronc busting behind: "Ridin' them old bronc horses was about the worst."

Nevertheless, it did seem glorious, exciting work to some, and Oklahoman June Cotton Martin Finn even fought for the opportunity to do it. Having grown up with ranch work, she believed by her early teens that she could do most anything a cowboy could, and she refused to let small stature and femaleness keep her out of the action. "I even talked Ben into letting me

break horses," she recalled, "and one of the horses I broke was one of the first ones they sent out there [for Hollywood movies]." She concedes that the work wasn't easy, but seemed to feel a deep sense of reward when it did pay off: "We had a lot of old hammerhead horses that wasn't worth a dime, but we had some that really were good work horses." A good horse is "one that's not lazy, one that will step on out. One that can turn real fast, because when you're headin' cattle, them cattle can turn right around." And that's just what a good peeler like June produced: first-rate cow ponies.

Most other cowboy chores appear far less romantic than the images we find in pulp fiction, novels, and films. They demanded skill, know-how, indefatigable patience—not to mention nerves of steel—and yet brought very little pay and even less prestige and appreciation. Jack Rollinson, who worked in Wyoming in the late 1890s, described butchering, one of many prosaic chores: "It took quite a knack to do a good job of butchering on the ground, as many a range man knows. We soon had the beef lying on its hide,

Below: *"Chester Byers roping, Pendleton, Oregon." Photographed by Ralph R. Doubleday, circa 1935.*

already skinned loose from the carcass. We used an ax to quarter it. We were within but a short distance of camp, so we carried the quarters in ourselves, as both our gentle horses objected decidedly to packing the bloody, freshly killed meat."[14]

Cowboys also had to keep a sharp eye out for cattle in trouble on the range, which meant basically riding around the same terrain again and again, day after day. William Owens, born in 1863, described the routine at one ranch he worked on in the Southwest, where cattle often got stuck in bogs, especially after it had rained. "We were kept busy riding the range looking out for bogged and crippled critters, also, rustlers. When we located a bogged critter the lariat was tied to the animal and fastened to the horn of the saddle, then the hoss [or sometimes two] did the pulling."

The roundups that seem such an exciting adventure to us modern folk provided the cowboy with a little exciting change of pace as well. Generally carried out only once or twice a year, roundups brought together cowboys from neighboring ranches to sort out and brand each ranch's cattle, which roamed freely (and mixed together) out on the plains. Roundups required a whole 'nother set of skills that cowboys got to practice only rarely, and gave

the cowboys a glimpse of new, fresh faces and a chance to visit with old friends—a rare pleasure on the isolated frontier. Roundups were also typically followed by ranch games and competitions, cowboy sporting events, picnics, parties, dances, and other sorts of country fun.

Throughout the West, and especially in Texas, "biggest" has long been a preoccupation. So where and when did the West's biggest roundup take place? According to Wyoming sources, they gathered nearly two hundred thousand cattle during one roundup. Ed Lemmon counters that such a figure actually represented the work of fifteen separate roundups. Lemmon bossed an 1897 roundup in South Dakota that brought together into one operation five roundups, fifteen wagons and crews, three hundred cowboys, and forty-five thousand cattle.[15] Like the host of the first rodeo, the site of the largest roundup remains contested, for a cowboy's tale was often taller than his

Breakfast on the Roundup. Famous cowboy artist C. M. Russell is 3rd man from left sitting in front row. Utica, Montana in background. Judith Roundup, early 1880s.

roundup was big. It is certain, though, that there were quite a few "biggies" back in the golden days.

Texan Ed Rawlings well described a typical roundup, spring or fall, of the late nineteenth century. Area ranches cooperated, each sending riders and outfits to a central location. A general boss sent "a bunch of riders out in every direction. They'd drive in all the cattle they could find to a central place, then each outfit would cut his stuff and hold it 'til all had been rounded up. The calves were branded, too. It took maybe a month or six weeks to complete a big round-up where there was lots of range to cover."

In addition to the obvious riding, herding, and roping, there were other, less well-known skills for a cowhand to cultivate on a roundup. In 1949, South Dakota cowboy Duncan Emrich recalled that, for as long as he could remember, "cowboys prided themselves on their ability to read brands and earmarks

DORIS HAYNES ON "BUSTER" LIVINGSTON, (DOUBLEDAY) ROUND-UP

quickly, not as simple an attainment on the open range, with moving cattle, as it seems on the printed page. With many head of several ranches gathered into the same herd at roundup time, with inevitable strays from distant ranges, it was the 'lettered' puncher who could pick up and sing out the correct brand and marking and identify the owner."

After sorting out each ranch's cattle, branding was the second task that constituted a central activity at any roundup. Especially on the open range, ranchers had to brand livestock—mostly that year's newborn calves—to show who owned which animals. Despite its seeming simplicity, there was a science to branding, and it took more brains and brawn than simply poking a cow with a hot rod if the brander didn't want to get kicked. In his memoir, *Excerpt from Cowboy Life in Texas: Or, 27 Years a Mavrick!*, W. S. James explained an important bit of cowboy expertise: "The difference in holding a horse and cow down is that you must hold the horse's front legs or head on the ground, because he never gets up behind first but throws his front feet

Above: *"Doris Haynes on "Buster" at the Livingston Round-Up, Livingston," Montana. Photographed by Ralph R. Doubleday, circa 1945.*

Below: *Six cowboys branding cattle in South Dakota. Photographed by John C. H. Grabill, 1891.*

out and then gets up; the cow on the contrary gets up directly the reverse, gets up on her hind feet first, therefore you must hold her down by the tail. The horse is easily choked down but it is almost an impossibility to choke a cow down."

Besides simply distinguishing between one ranch's cattle and another, brands served to deter rustlers, who would steal the cattle and take them into town to sell. The *Denver Republican* (December 13 and 14, 1892) reported an example on the South Dakota ranges that proves rustling was no mere piddling concern: "Five hundred head of cattle have been run off the Little Missouri valley in Billings County in the last six months. They are driven into the Bad Lands, where they cannot be found, and are sold off in small bunches." The following day, the paper reported at least a partial victory in a shootout between cowboys and the rustlers.

continued on page 98

Below: Six cowboys branding cattle in South Dakota. Photographed by John C. H. Grabill, 1891.

To rope the steers in rapid flight,

In round up is their keen delight.

With burning irons and steady hand,

On every calf they place a brand.

"The Cowboys," by Harry Ellard. 1899.[16]

"Known by their brand." Cattle being branded by three cowboys. Photographed by F. M. Steele, circa 1905.

Below: *Al Wise branding a Texas cow with a "W." Photographed by Solomon D. Butcher in Callaway, Custer County, Nebraska, in 1903. The horse is "Blue," noted by the photographer as the best cow pony of his day.*

Since brands obviously did not discourage all rustlers, ranchers had to employ a variety of additional tactics in order to protect their livelihood—and their cowboys' lives. They formed stockmen's organizations and hired professional gunmen to hunt down rustlers … and even planted spies. Tom Horn, who did just such work for the Wyoming Cattle Grower's Association, earned $500 for each suspected rustler that he shot and killed from ambush. In 1901, he became one of the best-known gunmen working as a "regulator" or "cattle detective" when the case of a fourteen-year-old boy who was shot and killed near Iron Mountain, Wyoming was publicized. The historical record casts doubts upon Horn's guilt, but a jury nonetheless convicted him of the

murder, and he died at the end of a rope on November 20, 1903. The shooting was most likely a case of mistaken identity: the gunman probably meant to kill the boy's rustler father.

In some areas, such as "No-Man's-Land" (the Oklahoma Panhandle), vigilante "justice" often prevailed when a pursuit finally came to a head. As a youth, African-American cowboy Matthew "Bones" Hooks experienced vigilante justice firsthand. Born in 1867 in Orangeville, Texas, he became a skilled bronco buster early in life, eventually hiring on as horse wrangler for two white cattlemen tending a herd. Unbeknownst to Hooks, the herd had been stolen. Vigilantes hanged the other two men and placed a noose around Hooks' neck. One of the vigilantes, "Skillety Bill" Johnson (so called because he worked for the Frying Pan Ranch) spoke up for Hooks. He argued that the callow youth probably did not know he had hired on with rustlers. "A red-haired man astride a limb of the tree gave the rope around my neck a rough jerk," Hooks vividly recalled, "and said, 'Aw, come on, let's get it over with,' but Skillety Bill saved my life." The vigilantes relented, and Hooks lived to tell the tale.

Above: *Some of the cowboys from the F. D. W. Ranch pose on a tree trunk somewhere in the plains country, possibly Texas or Oklahoma. Photographed by W. D. Harper, circa 1904.*

.....384 F. Gone Over the Big Divide.

Left: *"Gone Over the Big Divide." Cowboy kneeling at bedside of dead partner, banjo on table. Photographed by T.W. Ingersoll in St. Paul, Minnesota, circa 1902.*

Opposite: *"How to read brands." Arizona Highways, November 1960, page 5.*

The dangerous work and harsh conditions—not to mention the occasional violence—to which cowboys were regularly subjected demanded they be tough, brave, and somewhat foolhardy. Whoever didn't have those qualities when he signed on learned them right quick. Cowboys could usually depend on their horses and partners to help them through hard times, but they knew that there would be situations in which even their fierce loyalty would not suffice. The frontier was not only unpredictable, but often lonely, and if problems arose while out on the range, help could be hours or days away, so it was the cowboy's reliance upon himself that had to see him through the most troublesome predicaments. Tom Massey, of San Angelo, Texas, recounted an accident suffered by George Bright when the young cowboy's horse stepped in a hole and fell. Bright was knocked unconscious and suffered a broken leg, but when he came to, "[h]e took his knife, cut splints of mesquite sticks, tore up his undershirt and bound up his broken bones. The nearest human being was four miles away, so he started out crawling." He endured a thunderstorm the first night, but continued to crawl along the creek, packing mud onto his leg now and then in order to keep down the inflammation. When his friends finally found him, he was hatless, bootless, his clothes torn to shreds, and "covered with blisters as big as a dollar." Despite it all, George healed up nicely and lived to a ripe old age.

Such solitude prompted most cowboys to seek out the fellowship of other human beings, whether amongst their fellow cowhands, or by eventually retiring in order to start a family. A few men, however, relished the peace and quiet of living alone with nature. Mart Driver, for example, enjoyed the solitude of cowboy life in northwest Texas during the first decades of the twentieth century. He often lived alone in a small house out on the range. "Some men do not like to batch [live as bachelors]. They

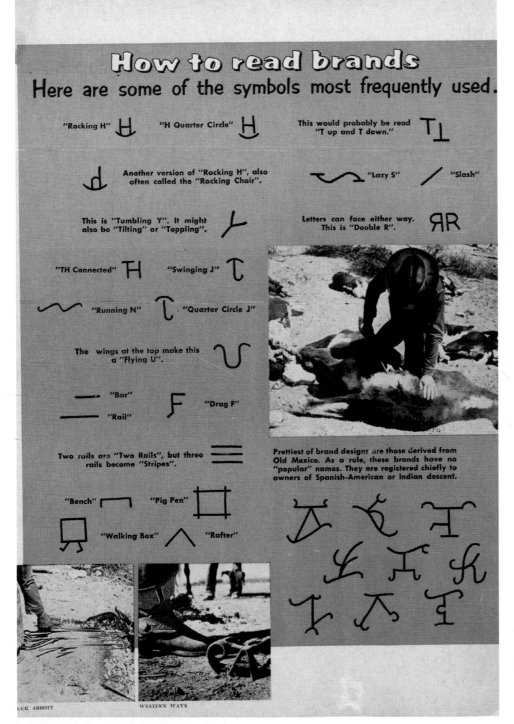

How to read brands
Here are some of the symbols most frequently used.

"Rocking H"

"H Quarter Circle"

This would probably be read "T up and T down."

Another version of "Rocking H", also often called the "Rocking Chair".

"Lazy S"

"Slash"

This is "Tumbling Y". It might also be "Tilting" or "Toppling".

Letters can face either way. This is "Double R".

"TH Connected"

"Swinging J"

"Running N"

"Quarter Circle J"

The wings at the top make this a "Flying U".

"Bar"

"Drag F"

"Rail"

Two rails are "Two Rails", but three rails become "Stripes".

Prettiest of brand designs are those derived from Old Mexico. As a rule, these brands have no "popular" names. They are registered chiefly to owners of Spanish-American or Indian descent.

"Bench"

"Pig Pen"

"Walking Box"

"Rafter"

UCK ABBOTT   WESTERN WAYS

complain of getting lonesome, but I never was that way. I never cared for any kind of games or dances. I never cared for a lot of company. I liked the camp life, liked being alone with just a big herd of cattle." After retiring, though, even Driver moved to town and got married.

Frontier demographics and the gender roles of the time tended to make the cowboy even lonelier. As proper Victorians, nineteenth-century ranchers strongly preferred to hire men to do horseback work, leaving the domestic chores of gardening, cooking, sewing, and childcare to women. As a result, far more men than women were hired to work on the ranch, and men vastly outnumbered women on the range. In fact, cowhands saw few women other than the rancher's wife and daughters, and they were usually indoors, rarely coming into contact with the cowhands. Because cowboys hardly ever talked with women—and because Victorian culture placed most women on an idealized plane, far beyond the ken of a smelly, poor "waddie"—they often exhibited considerable awkwardness and shyness around them, not unlike in the old B-western movies. In town, however, cowboys could consort (for a price) with dance hall girls and prostitutes.

The nature of gender relations and women's role on the ranch were nevertheless highly dependent upon social class and fluctuating

Above: *Rodeo performers pose in their costumes, including ten gallon hats, boots, and embroidered dresses. Among the group are: Ber Kirnan, Prarie Rose, Mable Strickland, Princis Mohawk, Ruth Roach, Kittie Canutt, and Prarie Lillie. Bleachers are in the background. Photographed by Ralph R. Doubleday, circa 1921.*

economic conditions. In fact, it was really only upper class women who were able to—and fully expected to—fulfill the Victorian ideal *all* of the time. Elmer E. Brown, who edited a small newspaper in Beaver, No-Man's-Land (Oklahoma), described the social conventions to which such "privileged" women were subject: "The cowgirl did not exist. The young women did not go cavorting over the prairies astride bucking bronchos. . . . It would have seemed exceedingly immodest for a young woman to get astride a horse wearing any sort of riding habit." Any woman doing so, warned Brown, "would have been classed as a bawdy house character, and every home on the plains would have been closed to her."

Such rigid gender restrictions did not extend to the lower social classes, and on small family ranches everyone had to pitch in regardless of Victorian gender roles. These roles were also temporarily set aside on most all ranches during and just after the Civil War, owing to the lack of available men. Texan W. F. Cude remembered that, in the post-war devastation of 1866, the Weaver family lived about thirty miles from Oakville in south Texas. Their two grown girls "would assist their father in hunting cattle, and carried their pistols with them wherever they went. They had a pack of hounds and hunted with them."[17]

Many women learned to love not just a woman's ranch life, but also the rough and dirty work of the men. In the mid-1880s, Alabama-born Mabel Luke Madison and her husband James moved from Texas to New Mexico. James worked for a time on shares, receiving some cash and taking the rest in calves from his employer, rancher Oliver Lee. James and Mabel soon accumulated enough cattle to begin their own J-M Ranch, located fourteen miles from Alamogordo. "I liked ranch life right from the start," Mabel recalled, "for I rode the range with Jim, learned to cook and eat chuck-wagon food and to ride and rope with the best of them."

Below: *Dehorning with Bigum Bradley, "Marlboro Ad Cowboy." Photographed by E. Helbig, 1984.*

Copyright 1903
by Adams
Patson M.T. Montana Girl.

Above: *"Montana Girl." Woman in cowgirl attire on horseback. Photographed circa 1909.*

Quite a few women became accomplished riders and herded cattle, even earning the respect and admiration of their male counterparts. Earl Horne, of Travis County, Texas, termed Billy O'Brian, a ranch foreman's daughter, "the best woman rider I ever knew.... She'd catch her mount in the mornings, same as the other riders. She was shore a good hand too." W. O. Eubanks, of Comanche County, Texas, deemed Dessa Calloway "the best lady rider I ever knew. She could ride horses and work cattle like a man. She could ride broncs or anything. She learned to ride on her father's ranch." Georgie Sicking, who worked her adult life as a cowhand and rancher in Nevada during the twentieth century, recorded many of her adventures in poems that she presents at gatherings throughout the West. She took part in her last roundup in 2002, at the still-youthful age of 81—talk about a love of the cowgirl's life!

In the 1880s, two factors combined to tip the flourishing ranching industry from its peak: the source of investment and, quite simply, the weather. In the course of this single decade, cowhands and ranchers enjoyed some of the greatest, most glorious trail rides and roundups that we associate with the golden age of cowboying. They endured some of the hardest, most drastic changes the cattle industry has ever undergone and some of the most devastating winters the West has ever seen. Perhaps most importantly, though, they learned crucial lessons about raising cattle out on the great American plains, about adjustment to circumstances, and about survival. Those who couldn't keep up dropped out of the business altogether, while those who did learn to adapt went on to shape the cattle industry into what we know today.

The first factor was the wealthy outsiders who, attracted by the great potential for profit, began eyeing the Western ranching ventures beginning in the mid-1880s. The most unlikely of cowboys—blue-blooded Europeans from royal and aristocratic families—suddenly became part of the rough-and-tumble Western American ranching scene. Scottish and British financiers invested most heavily: British investors alone pumped an estimated $40 million into the range cattle industry.

Distant and foreign as they were, these men could clearly have no understanding of daily life on an American ranch. Their vision for the Wild West was a land organized on a new corporate model, one in which profits and efficiency were maximized at any cost. To achieve those ends, they sometimes sent European managers utterly innocent of Western life to run their cattle operations, many of whom displayed a haughty contempt for their lower-class employees—the cowboys. Some of the European operations even imposed new, restrictive rules and regulations that, though they might have

Above: *Woman posing in cowgirl outfit, holding revolver, seated on table with playing cards. Photographed circa 1909.*

Branding at Monument Lake VVN Ranch 1898. J.A. Oden Roping

Above: *"Branding at Monument Lake VVN Ranch, J.A. Oden Roping." Eastman Kodak Company, 1898.*

endeared the foreigners to some, certainly won them no points with the freedom-loving cowboy.

With their eyes solely on output and profit, these European investors began overstocking their ranges. The number and size of herds and ranches exploded upon the Western plains, often pushing into marginal grazing lands. What they did not foresee in those glorious days of cowboy capitalism was that this would naturally cause the price of cattle to plummet. What perhaps they could not have foreseen was that even the great wide West has limited resources and a maximum capacity. That, however, they would soon learn as the grass ran out and the frost came down.

From 1885 through 1887, a series of extremely harsh winter storms killed millions of cattle on the Great Plains. An estimated three-fourths of northern range cattle perished. One writer described the scene in the Dakota Badlands: "Blizzard after blizzard, storm after storm shrank and wasted the splendid herds to ghostly shadows; the place was a boneyard. Thousands after thousands of fine cattle lay down and died of sheer starvation. Without mercy that dreadful winter clung on until the late dawning of spring saw only a few wasted shadows where before had ranged splendid herds." Montana cowboy artist Charlie Russell captured the pathos of the time in his famous painting *Last of the 5000*. Following what came to be known as "the great die-up," in most of the West massive roundups and long trail drives passed quickly from history into mythology.

These successive brutal winters killed the spirits and credit of many ranchers and many, but not all, gave up. Those who survived were the ones who learned the lessons of that tragedy and began making the necessary arrangements to prevent such losses in the future: they adjusted herd sizes to match the carrying capacity of the grasslands, began growing hay to feed livestock during winter months, and they started to build those infamous fences around their lands. Such fundamental changes had a domino effect, requiring many other adaptations in their wake: ranchers were now forced to invest in

Above: *"Reading the news." Two cowboys reading some papers next to the "USM" postbox near the LS Ranch in Texas. Photographed by Erwin E. Smith, circa 1908.*

plows in order to be able to farm properly; fences separated cattle from their water sources, so windmills had to be built and maintained; others even began diversifying their livestock, especially through the acquisition of sheep—a completely different type of ranching altogether.

This shift from open-range ranching and long trail drives to fenced ranges naturally procured many changes in the cowboy's life as well. He was, after all, the working hands of the ranch, and so he not only implemented those changes, but spent a considerable amount of time maintaining them thereafter: fences had to be tended and repaired, hay had to be cut each season and hauled to racks, and windmills were constantly breaking. Dave Hoffman, born in Avon, Missouri, in 1900, described the cowboy's work about 1917: "After the fence was completed, one rider rode the fence line constantly, looking for breaks. The small breaks he would repair, and the large breaks were fixed by the repair crew." The work required simple tools (a hammer, pliers, and staples) but very long hours. Mart Driver, who worked on the Spade Ranch in Lamb County (northwestern Texas) from 1914 through 1928, spent less time on fences, but more on windmills: "Sometimes I was punching cattle and sometimes I was repairing windmills. There were 50 windmills on the ranch and for two years I spent most of my time keeping those mills up." While most cowboys were not fond of the new menial tasks, it was the prospect of someday having to learn to farm that was usually the breaking point—the mere thought of it could even provoke a cattleman to violence. A verse from an old Western ballad, "Goodbye You Old Dry Landers," expressed that anger quite gently, by comparison:

I was raised on a ranch in Montana,
All I know is to rope an old cow;
I never did work on a sheep ranch,
And damned if I'd follow a plow.

Not only did the work on ranches become more predictable and routinized than it had been on the open range, but, to the cowboy, the range itself seemed to be metamorphosing into an unrecognizable sight right before his eyes: wheat fields and other crops quickly replaced the natural long grasses that once fed huge herds of cattle, and the newly tamed landscape suddenly was dotted by as many sheep as cows—and even the cows weren't the same. In 1885, Charles A. Siringo humorously described what he (correctly) predicted all the cross-breeding on ranches would soon mean for the cowboy: "Cattle are becoming so tame from being bred up with short horns that it requires but very little skill and knowledge to be a Cow-boy. I believe the day is not far distant when cow-boys will be armed with prod-poles to punch the cattle on their way—instead of firearms."

It's no wonder that some old-time cowhands began to feel a little out of place in those strange surroundings. And yet the changes didn't stop with the landscape or even with the cattle. First railroads, then motor vehicles spread through the West, rendering not just the cowboy's traditional ranch work, but also his trail riding, wholly obsolete. For many an adventure-loving cattleman, it was the last straw: they opted to move on to other ventures. L. M. Cox of Brownwood, Texas reflected on those days in an interview during the late 1930s: "We don't have ranches any more; just windmill and pasture projects. These dipping vats, bah! We used to have to dip some of the punchers but never the cattle. I tried for awhile to fall in with their new-fangled ways but

continued on page 112

*The Horse Wrangler. Photographed by
Erwin E. Smith, circa 1910.*

I hate to see the wire fence

    A-closin' up the range;

And all this fillin' in the trail

With people that is strange.

We fellers don't know how to plough,

Nor reap the golden grain;

But to round up steers and brand the cows

To us was allus plain.

"Bronc Peeler's Song," popular tune.

"Settlers taking the law in their own hands, cutting 15 miles of the Brighton Ranch fence in 1885." Photographed by Solomon D. Butcher, circa 1900.

Above and Opposite: *Modern-day cowboys, El Reno, Oklahoma, 2004.*

when they got to roundin' up and herdin' in Ford cars I thought it was about time for a first class cowman to take out, so I guess I'm what you'd call retired."

While these changes alienated the majority of cowmen at the time, their successors would not just get used to them—they would never know anything else. There is one chore, however, that binds all cattlemen of all eras and regions together, and that is their common battle against the ever-unpredictable weather. Even fences and windmills and hay have not been able to completely cut the losses of what is necessarily an outdoor business. Throughout the twentieth century, harsh storms and unusually cold winters plagued the cowboy as it always has and must. During the "Big Winter" of 1906–07, storms raged from November through May, and temperatures plummeted to fifty below. A blizzard blown in from the northwest heralded that sudden disaster, covering every last blade of grass within the first hour. Ike Blasingame recalled that "[t]he hungry hordes [of cattle] crossed the drifted-under fences and level-full ravines, until eventually thousands crowded into the Little Bend of the Missouri River, below Cheyenne River Agency. . . . Cattle that came in lower down missed this bend

and landed on the Cheyenne—all of them starving, eating brush, willow sticks, anything that stuck up above the snow that buried everything for months.... Men cut down the smaller trees along the streams so stock could eat the bark and twigs in the tops."

The new ranch also faced new problems, brought about by everything from global competition and changing market trends to diets fads and "mad cow" hysteria.

And of course, technology plays no small role on the modern ranch: brawny pickup trucks are now as common on ranches as quarter horses; cattle herding is often done using helicopters and ATVs (all-terrain vehicles); computers have replaced the old knotted strings that once kept track of livestock, feed, weather patterns, and other variables in ranching; the Internet provides information on cattle prices as well as a place to trade

Above: *Modern-day cowboy, El Reno, Oklahoma, 2004.*

Opposite: *OKC West Livestock Market, El Reno, Oklahoma, 2004.*

animals; and fax machines, cell phones, and satellite dishes have replaced battery-operated radios. According to a Texas cowboy, though, the biggest difference between the cowboys of today and yesterday lies simply in the number of hours spent in the saddle: "These days we've got pickups and trailers, and in the old days they wore out more horses and saddle leather." Indeed, on the ranches that now host ecotours, wildlife viewing, and horseback trips to supplement income, ranchers often wrangle more dudes than they do cattle.

Even the rustlers have adopted more sophisticated methods of perpetrating their sinister old crime. Retired cowboy John H. Fuller explains that "[t]he rustler today cuts the line fence, drives in, and loads a few critters that he hauls to town. In most cases, the critters are killed before the ramrod [ranch manager] knows he has lost any cattle." Autumn, when many ranchers pen up cattle for fattening, now marks prime time for rustlers. And when beef prices spike, as they did in 2003, rustlers, sometimes driving eighteen-wheelers that can hold fifty cattle, cut into the herds and profits, just as they did a

century ago. Modern technology seems to have only made the cow-thief bolder—after all, it's easier to back a trailer up to a pen than to chase down cattle in a pasture.

On the other hand, the vigilante "justice" that once reigned in the Wild West has been supplanted by organized law enforcement. These days the good guys respond not with bounty hunts and shoot-outs, but with helicopters, DNA fingerprinting, and a computerized livestock database that traces missing cattle. And to discourage rustling in the first place, ranchers now embed transponders in ear tags or in a small glass vile placed beneath the animal's skin. In spite of all the new technologies and fancy gadgets, it's still the old-fashioned brand, permanent and difficult to alter, that serves as the rancher's first line of defense.

In a letter from August 14, 1922, artist Charles M. Russell described what he—and many other cowboys of his time—perceived to be their fate: "The barbed

wire and plow made the cow puncher History, and the onley place hes found now is on paper." While it is true that most people today get their ideas about cowboys from novels, movies, and art, real "flesh-and-blood" ranch hands do still ride the Western ranges. And yet, it is clear that the golden age of ranching and cowboying is behind us. That time, with all its hardships and setbacks, dangers and uncertainties, still inspires nostalgia in the ranch people of today as much as it does in the general public that often knows only of its glory and adventure.

Opposite: *18-wheelers, El Reno, Oklahoma, 2004.*

Above: *Hair-clipping at Express Ranches, Yukon, Oklahoma, 2004.*

Above: *Cattle sale at OKC Livestock Market, El Reno, Oklahoma, 2004.*

Even with all their modern comforts and conveniences, modern cowhands often long for what President Theodore Roosevelt wistfully described as "the great free ranches, with their barbarous, picturesque, and curiously fascinating surroundings." For never having a chance to know and love the beauty of that life that he so thoroughly relished, Roosevelt expressed more pity for us than for the cowboy of his day, who personally loved and lost: "We who have felt the charm of the life, and have exulted in its abounding vigor and its bold, restless freedom, will not only regret its passing for our own sakes, but

Below: *Theodore Roosevelt ranching in the Dakota Badlands. Photographed in the 1880s.*

must also feel real sorrow that those who come after us are not to see, as we have seen, what is perhaps the pleasantest, healthiest, and most exciting phase of American existence."[18]

UP THE TRAIL

The golden age of cowboy life began just after the Civil War, a conflict that took most able-bodied adult males away from Texas. In their absence, cattle herds proliferated and ran wild. With few people to care for them and with very limited market outlets thanks to Union blockades, the number of cattle in Texas increased mightily. Texan George Sanders, too young to join the Confederate forces, recalled those days: "With a few old men, boys and Negroes, we worked the range from Karnes County to Nueces County, branding calves for our neighbors who were away at war, and dividing mavericks with those who had cattle on our range."

After the Confederate surrenders at Appomattox, Virginia, and Bennett Place, North Carolina, in April 1865, Texans returned to their ranches to find a huge oversupply of cattle that rendered them largely worthless. "But they'd be worth something up north," somebody reasoned. That hope spawned the great trail drives north from Texas to Abilene, Wichita, Dodge City, and many other famed cow towns.

Texans actually began driving small herds of cattle out of the state to more profitable markets in the 1840s. Most of the animals were sold to Midwestern farmers, who fattened them up for sale at local markets. Along Western trails, cattlemen took up livestock trading with emigrants bound for Oregon and California, and learned from their own migrations that cattle could survive northern winters. Many of the northern plains states recognize these early "road ranchers" as the fathers of their cattle industries: Richard Grant in Fort Hall, Idaho, Lancaster P. Lupton in Colorado, and Granville Stuart in western Montana, all of whom traded livestock with

Above: *"Ready to break camp." Group of cowboys on cattle drive ready to break camp, somewhere in Colorado. The picture shows a man on horseback with chaps and lasso attached to saddle; four men standing in front of canvas tent, one possibly holding a branding iron; four men and a boy lounging around smoldering campfire with cookpot hanging from metal rods; two packhorses being loaded; horse with brand on right leg (Circle X); cooking pots, buckets, wash basins, rolled sleeping bags. The photographer's shadow and camera on tripod with drape are visible in the right foreground. Photographed by L. C. McClure, Denver, Colorado, 1900–1920.*

Page 120: *Buffalo grazing along the Madison River, Montana, 2001.*

Page 121: *Cowboy in wooly chaps [woolies] shaving at wagon. Unknown photographer, circa 1910.*

Below: *Circle roundup in Valley County, Montana. Tom Morris on horse. Photographed by Charles E. Morris, Chinook, Montana.*

passers-through, are considered the first "ranchers" in their respective states.

The 1840s also saw the first recorded large cattle drive when, in 1846, Edward Piper moved 1,000 head from Texas to Ohio. Thereafter, the number of cattle trailed north from Texas varied from year to year, and consequently the number of cowboys hired rose and fell. The effect of the Civil War upon the cowboy's work is reflected in the statistics: In 1867, only 35,000 cattle made the trek out of the Lone Star State, but two years later that figure increased ten-fold. The high-water mark came in 1871—right smack in the middle of the "golden age" of cowboying—when cowboys moved 600,000 cattle up the trail. A decade later the total fell back down to 250,000.

Cowboys rode many famous trails as they pushed herds of cattle west and north from Texas to California, Colorado, Wyoming, Montana, the Dakotas, and eventually into British Columbia and Alberta, Canada. Certainly, though, no trail became more famous than that named for Tennessee-born Jesse Chisholm (1805–1868). In 1865, he laid out a trail from Wichita, Kansas to the Indian reservation known as the Wichita-Caddo Agency (now Anadarko,

continued on page 126

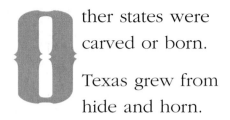ther states were carved or born.

Texas grew from hide and horn.

Other states are long and wide.

Texas is a shaggy hide.

"Cattle," by Berta Hart. Circa 1931.

Crawford Trail Herd, No-Man's-Land. On the back of the photograph is written:"The best trail outfit that ever drove a herd from South Texas they always got the cattle through regardless of many personal dangers. Crawford Trail herd, no mans land, near Beaver City, 1887."

Oklahoma). Soon Texas cattle drivers, traders, and freight wagons were using the 200-mile route that ran through southwestern Oklahoma and extending it both south- and northward. Eventually the entire journey, from San Antonio, Texas to Abilene, Kansas, covered about 800 miles. Herds originating in south Texas covered 1,000 miles.

Throughout the nineteenth century, cowboys continued to blaze trails as they became necessary. Herders developed the Western Trail in response to the increasingly vocal—and sometimes violent—opposition of eastern Kansas farmers to the transit of Texas Longhorns through their lands. In addition to the loss of grass and water, they feared that the Texas cattle would spread dangerous foot-and-mouth disease to their animals. Hence the Western Trail connected to Dodge City instead of Wichita, a path that deliberately avoided eastern Kansas, and it eventually pushed all the way north to Fort Buford in western Dakota Territory. Charles Goodnight and Oliver Loving blazed a trail to move their cattle from west Texas through eastern New Mexico and then on to Colorado and Cheyenne, Wyoming. That route became famous in popular culture owing to the novel and television miniseries *Lonesome Dove*. The Shawnee Trail forked to the east of the Chisholm, branching to railheads in Kansas City, Sedalia, and St. Louis, Missouri. John Bozeman opened a trail from central Wyoming north into Montana in the mid-1860s. Vaqueros and cowboys also moved cattle between Oregon and California and north from Oregon to British Columbia, Canada.

How does one move a herd of hundreds or thousands of wild and semi-wild Longhorns up a trail for months? *With great difficulty!* Simply getting cattle to move from their accustomed range proved an arduous challenge. As a teenager in the 1880s, W. L. Rhodes helped trail a herd a hundred miles from Kaufman to Throckmorton County, Texas. "The first 50 miles of any trail drive is always the hardest," he said, "because the cattle want to break back to the country they're used to. We sure had to haze a many a one back before we got the herd used to moving." Once on the move and away from the accustomed range, storms, alkali dust, river crossings, quicksand, dry water holes, prairie fires, rustlers, Indian raids, and of course, stampedes awaited the herders.

On The Chisholm Trail, *by Paul Moore, Chisholm Trail Heritage Center, Duncan, Oklahoma.*

Stampedes were the most common obstacle on trail drives—and potentially the most destructive. W. A. Tinney, born in Texas in 1863 and already on the trail by age eleven, noted the average cowboy's expectations by way of a most unusual exception: "A peculiar thing about my first trail drive was that there wasn't a single stampede. Now, stampedes are a part of trail drives, and were expected at any time by the cowpoke on to his job." George Saunders' first drive north, on the other hand, was much closer to typical: "[T]he steers were very wild, and for the first 200 miles of our journey, they stam-

peded day and night." Almost anything could spook cattle: the flare of a match, a clap of thunder, a gust of wind. … W. L. Rhodes, on a drive south of Graham, Texas, even experienced this oddity: "A couple of house cats went to fighting, and stampeded that herd: House cats! They sure caused us a heap of trouble, because we were two days rounding that herd up again."

Foul weather was usually the sinister force behind a stampede, and anyone who has sojourned on the plains knows that foul weather is always just a breeze away. Sudden, severe thunder-, wind-, rain-, hail-, snow-,

Opposite: *"Santa Fe Trail Tracks, 1822–1872." Dodge City, Kansas.*

Above: *Buffalo crossing the Madison River, Montana, 2001.*

and dust storms, tornadoes, and even flash floods make this region one of the most fickle and unpredictable in the world. As G. W. Mills discovered near Ft. Dodge on the Arkansas River, the weather was enough to torment the perpetually outdoors cowboy all by itself: "About two o'clock in the evening, the awfulest hailstorm came up a man ever saw. The hailstones nearly beat us to death; it knocked over jackrabbits like taking them off with a rifle. It even killed a few yearlings and many fleet antelopes, but the cow hands had to stick to their posts, although we nearly froze to death."[19] J. R. Walkup suffered a similar wind-, rain-, and hailstorm in Wyoming that killed twenty Longhorn cattle. "The hailstones were so large that the trail drivers

continued on page 133

129

ill we reached the open plains, everything went well,

And then them cattle turned in and dealt us merry hell.

They stampeded every night that came and did it without fail,

Oh, you know we had a circus as we all went up the trail.

"John Garner's Trail Herd," author unknown. 1908.[20]

Wyoming cattle drive, Evanston, Wyoming. Photographed by Baker & Johnston, circa 1885.

in order to escape serious injury had to dismount and unsaddle their horses and place the saddles over their heads, while the six thousand longhorns surged away before the storm and scattered over the country." Such was the cowboy's rule of thumb: wild winds never blew alone, but invariably took the cattle with them.

Stampedes did not merely represent an inconvenience and loss of time and money—they could be deadly. The *Denver Republican* (August 13, 1892) described the dire result of a stampede that occurred near Bannock Butte, Idaho, in which two cowboys raced to the head of a herd in order to stop the steers from charging off the edge of a cliff. "Their horrified companions saw them swept off the cliff as the maddened animals, unable to stop, rushed over. Three hundred and sixty-one cattle were forced off the cliff and fell seventy-nine feet. The bodies of the two cowboys were found dreadfully mangled."[21] Everyone breathed a sigh of relief if a stampede ended without loss of life to man or beast. More often than not, though, only the cowboys managed to emerge unscathed, and the ensuing chore of cleaning up the damage was nearly as unpleasant as the stampede itself. Ed Lemmon explained: "I was never in a stampede where a man or a horse was hurt—and I was in all kinds of stampedes in the fifty-three years I followed the Longhorns. But the bad part of that one was the big job we had skinning the dead cattle, and then the authorities made us bury the carcasses."[22]

A cowboy's dependence on the support of his fellow cowhands was matched only by his reliance on the horse he rode, and there was no better test of a horse's reliability than a stampede. A good horse managed to stay calm, trust in his rider, and follow his orders. A bad horse or, as George Saunders called them, "wild, pitching rascals," could frighten, lose control, and throw his rider to the ground—right in the midst of the stampeding herd. Cowboys were also not all star-riders, as the glorified legends would have it, and innocent falls were common as well. In truth, in the midst of the chaos that was a stampede, even the best of horses and riders sometimes relied on plain old luck. Dave McCrohan narrowly escaped death when he fell from his horse in front of stampeding cattle. "I disrobed my slicker, began shaking and whirling it into the air; this turned the cattle, and was all that saved me and my horse from being stamped into the earth." In the early 1890s, two riders from the CSJ outfit in Indian Territory [Oklahoma] did not fare as well. After

Cowboys trailing weaned calves to Whit Ranch. Photographed circa 1933.

night had fallen, a sudden wind and thunderstorm spooked the herd. Kansas-born John H. Fuller recalled that, about six miles from the origin of the stampede, "we found Slim stomped to death. No doubt his hoss hit a hole, and Slim took a spill among the running critters. Red was found a short piece yonder from Slim with a cracked leg bone that he got from a spill."

Given the prevalence and many potential dangers of stampedes, "waddies" (another term for cowboys) spent considerable time devising preventative strategies. According to David McCrohan, who cowboyed during the 1870s, "if the herd got restless we would always sing to quiet

them; a stampede was often prevented by the singing cowboy." Henry Young even offered one plausible tactic for reducing the likelihood of stampedes by controlling the make-up of the herd itself: "During my entire stay with the outfit [CA Bar Ranch in west Texas], we never had a bad stampede. The reason for that was that Adair kept his herd cleaned of beef critters, so there never was many old steers. The herd was mostly breeding cows and yearlings, and those critters are not so quick on the run. It is the steers, a year old and up, that are always looking for an excuse to run." Alas, most of the time, a cowboy could not choose what sort of cattle he herded.

Ralph Stockton with turned-out spring yearlings. The snow got so deep that he brought them back to feed on hay. Pitchfork Ranch, Meeteetsee 1920.

The landscape out on the plains presented its own challenges. In spite of the relatively extensive network of rivers that crisscrosses most of the West, cowboys were generally reared in arid environments and so never learned to swim. River crossings were beset with hazards, from swirling currents and flash floods to water moccasin nests and quicksand. On top of it all, the cattle and horses knew well enough to fear the crossings, which merely multiplied the difficulties of the cowboy's job. Texan Ed Rawlings, born in 1864, described one difficult crossing on the swollen Canadian River that separates Texas and Oklahoma. First they let the water recede, and then they moved the animals to the far (Oklahoma) shore. "As they came out of the water they walked into quicksand. We had to work fast to keep 'em from boggin' down. We lost some in spite of all we could

do. It was terrible to hear them bawlin' and almost screamin' for help as they went down."

Wherever there was water, there was bound to be trouble; but where there *wasn't* water, the result could be even worse. In his famous memoir, *Log of a Cowboy*, Andy Adams recounted the difficulties of controlling a trail herd, feverish with thirst. "We threw our ropes in their faces, and when this failed, we resorted to shooting; but in defiance of the fusillade and the smoke they walked sullenly through the line of horsemen across their front. Six-shooters were discharged so close to the leaders' faces as to singe their hair. . . . In a number of instances wild steers deliberately walked against our horses, and then for the first time a fact dawned on us that chilled the marrow in our bones—the herd was going blind."

Opposite: *Cattle in winter snowstorm. Photographed by Charles J. Belden..*

Above: *Chuck Curtis and cattle fording the Shoshone River near Cody, Wyoming. The bridge wouldn't hold them. In his time working, Chuck herded nearly 600 head— at $31 a head—across here to be shipped to California. Photographed by Charles J. Belden*

What Mother Nature didn't deal him in the way of dust, wind, and water, the cowboy's fellow frontier-dwellers often doled out by fire. Misunderstandings between cowboys and outsiders bred fear and suspicion, and so we find that much of the late nineteenth-century West was characterized by conflict between cattlemen and farmers. George Saunders explained that, on the Chisholm Trail, local cattle along the way sometimes mixed in the Texas road herds. "This caused lots of trouble between trail men and stockmen and farmers along the route, and led many of the latter to believe that all trail men were thieves." Mistrust and territoriality, combined in an environment of relative lawlessness, provoked defensiveness and even violence. "Many of the prairie fires," explained Mrs. Amanda Burks, who experienced such a fire on a drive in 1871, "were started by squatters on land who wanted to keep strangers away. They would plough a safety boundary around their stake and then set fire to the grass outside."[23]

Prairie fires constituted a major danger to humans and animals, wreaked havoc on land and property and, in the absence of modern fire-fight-

Above: *Winter cattle drive. Photographed by Charles J. Belden, 1920s.*

Opposite: *A herd of cattle moving across the plains. Photographed by Charles J. Belden between 1920 and 1940.*

ing equipment, took considerable time, energy, and manpower to extinguish. Living in western Oklahoma during the 1860s, James Childers joined all the cowhands from miles around to extinguish a prairie fire that extended over a front of 100 miles. Even with at least 1,000 men fighting the fire at any given time, it managed to spread 150 miles before they could bring it under control. Childers and the other cowhands employed a common means to fight the fire, making innovative use of the one thing they had in abundance: "The method we employed to fight a prairie fire was using green cow hides. We weighted the head and forefeet to hold the hide on the ground. A rope was tied to each of the hind feet part of the hide, and then a mounted cowboy took hold of each and dragged the hide over the fire. Thus most of the fire would be smothered."

Contrary to the many misconceptions of outsiders, the cowboy's code of honor—and difficult circumstances—demanded that he cooperate with and trust his fellow cowhands. It was in everybody's interest, as the case of James

Childers shows, to alleviate the danger and unpredictability of the environment in which Westerners found themselves. Thus we find that, in spite of the reputation of the West as "wild" and lawless, cowboys adhered to a certain set of rules that dictated (more or less) honorable behavior. Childers reported further that, while working in "No-Man's Land," an area particularly infamous for outbreaks of violence and mayhem, he recalled no instance of a cowboy being robbed. The hands stored their valuables in saddlebags, often left lying around the camp or chuck wagon, and yet "[w]e never feared that anyone would molest our money."

This was both extremely praiseworthy and not so surprising when one considers how much a cowboy probably had on him at any given time. Praiseworthy, because he earned so little that the temptation to get just a bit of extra cash somehow—anyhow—must have been nearly overwhelming at times. And still it's not surprising, because it's not like he could have gotten much out of any other cowboy, either. On average, cowboys on trail drives earned from $25 to $40 a month. Wranglers, who tamed and cared for the *remuda* (spare horses) received $50; cooks and ramrods (managers) $75; trail bosses earned $100 or more per month, and often received a bonus, sharing the profits from the drive. At the end of the trail, steers fetched $10 to $15 apiece and cows $7 to $10, making for a handsome profit, assuming minimal losses en route. Sometimes ranchers preferred

Above: Drifting Before The Storm, *by Frederic Remington. Circa 1904.*

Opposite: *Jack Rhodes on his horse in a blizzard at Pitchfork (Timber Creek) Meeteetsee, Wyoming. Photographed by Charles J. Belden, circa 1926–1927.*

to hire contract drovers, who moved the animals up the trail for $1 or $1.50 each.

Despite that handsome profit for his employer, the cowboy rarely felt bitterness about his low wages or work. "Employee theft" to get what one felt one "deserved" was nowhere near as talked about back then as it is today. The gap between rancher and cowhand was a great one, and yet the *Democratic Leader* (Cheyenne, January 11, 1885) reported that "the genuine cowboy of today is a faithful employee, who serves the interest of his principal with fidelity. . . . A certain sort of grit—the Western phrase is sand—is demanded."[24]

Such principles extended to interactions with women, who, despite the cowboys' isolation from the pressures of Victorian moral standards, were nevertheless treated with the respect and dignity that those standards prescribed. Though their presence was rare out on the range, those women who did come into close contact with cowboys usually expressed the utmost admiration for them. Mrs. Jack Miles, a ranchman's wife who was interviewed in the 1930s, put it well: "The old-fashioned cowboys were the finest fellows I ever knew, loyal and true in every respect and had the greatest respect for women. They would lay down their lives if necessary for a woman. They were congenial among themselves and would give their boss the best they had in them." When one considers how the cowboy could behave among men (and just think of his filthy mouth), it is easy to admire the discipline with which he restrained himself in mixed company.

A lady out on the trail might even find herself flattered and pampered precisely due to the rareness of feminine presence. Mrs. Amanda Burks, who accompanied her husband William F. on a drive in the spring of 1871, described her experience: "Being the only woman in camp, the men rivaled each other in attentiveness to me. They were always on the lookout for something to please me, a surprise of some delicacy of the wild fruit, or prairie chicken, or antelope tongue." [25]

During the early twentieth century, mechanized transportation rendered the great, long trail drives obsolete. First, railroad spurs connected more locations, thereby shortening the drives. A bit later, large trucks and trailers

XIT ("Ten-in-Texas") cowboys, members of a Texas Panhandle trail herd. Back row, left to right: Steve Beebe, Frank Freeland, Billy Wilson. Front row, left to right: John Flowers, Al (Alden) Denby, Tom McHenry, Dick Mabrey, Tony (last name unknown). Photographed by Wiley Brothers, Miles City, Montana, 1890.

connected locations not served by railroads. Some shorter cattle drives have survived: drive the back roads of Montana, Wyoming, or Nevada today and you might encounter cowboys driving a herd along the road, probably moving them from one fenced pasture to another. In Colorado, cowboys still make seasonal drives between summer mountain ranges and winter lowland pastures. Given modern labor costs, however, you'll more likely see large cattle trucks—with their stained and louvered aluminum sides, pronounced odor, and noisy, bawling load—carrying cattle from one place to another. Find the right dude or guest ranch and you, too, can participate in the rigors of a modern cattle drive, not unlike those of more than a century ago. Think *City Slickers*.

COWBOY FOOD & FUN

The cowboy generally enjoyed his breakfast well before sunrise, anytime from three to five in the morning. Supper came at day's end, either at the ranch or, when out on the trail, around the chuckwagon. These two main meals were typically prepared by the camp cook.

For the cowboy's meager mid-day meal—should he have time for one—a hastily eaten snack was the norm. A cowboy riding the range might carry in his saddlebags a few sourdough biscuits, some dried fruit, and beef jerky. He might also pack a frying pan to cook bacon and biscuits (time permitting) and, if he had a coffeepot, he would enjoy a cup or two of coffee.

Both on the trail and on the ranch, the cook—for better or worse—set the daily timetable and kept an outfit running. His essential role invested him with considerable power and earned him higher wages, as well as grudging respect from regular hands. Though men invariably worked as cooks on trail drives and on many ranches, cowboys readily acknowledged women to be superior cooks and looked forward to any meal cooked by one. Born in 1884, Texan Calvin Roberson worked as a cowboy in "Indian Territory" (Oklahoma) and Texas. He points up the rarity of female cooks on ranches: "The one

woman cook I knew while I worked there was said to be part Indian and was known to everyone as 'Flapjack Sally.' She was some bean slinger and wasn't afraid of hard work. I have heard that she could dress a wound or set a broken bone as well as any M. D. She was a great story teller and the Indian stories she could tell would make the hair rise up on a feller's head and stay up."

The cook's role at the very center of cowboy life demanded attention from every cowhand, and so we find that many cowboys' fondest memories of their cattle driving days feature their favorite cook and his best chuck. Henry Young enjoyed the meals at the CA Bar Ranch near Colorado City, Texas. He especially enjoyed it when the cook, nicknamed "Dog Face," would make "bean-hole beans." "Dog Face would dig a hole in the ground, line the hole with stone, then build a fire in the hole and keep it burning for several hours. Those stones would get piping hot, then the hole was ready for the beans. He put the beans into an iron kettle, with a tight cover, set it in the hole and covered it with sand." After several hours of slow cooking, "Dog Face" added bacon and molasses and served up large portions of the savory dish.

Page 144: *Modern cowboy cook at chuck wagon gathering, Oklahoma City, Oklahoma, 2004.*

Page 145: *Cowboys singing around the chuck wagon. Photographed by Charles J. Belden*

Opposite: *Chuck wagon and cook, circa 1963.*

Above: *Cowboys at the wagon, T-1, circa 1968.*

09273. COWBOYS AT LUNCH.

The isolation on ranches and the unpredictability of circumstances on the trail demanded considerable culinary ingenuity from the cowboy cook. Aside from "baking" in the ground in the absence of ovens, cooks learned to adapt whatever ingredients were on hand to their needs. To settle coffee grinds, for instance, eggshells floated in the kettle worked as well as any coffee filter does today. During the mid-twentieth century, Oklahoma cowboy Ray Holmes fondly remembered making ice cream on Sundays, with delicious toppings provided by

nature herself: wild strawberries, raspberries, or whatever other sweet, juicy treat the cowboys could find.[26] Wood is often hard to come by out on the largely treeless plains, and yet there is no shortage of buffalo chips—which is just what George Murray's cook used to bake his sourdough biscuits.

Under ideal circumstances, the cook was blessed with a wagon full of supplies as well as inexhaustible creativity, and his chuck was generally tasty and filling, even if it did lack variety. Two wagons often accompa-

A group of cowboys sit and eat a meal by a chuck wagon. Photographed by William H. Jackson, 1904.

nied a trail drive: one filled with bedrolls and personal belongings, the other—the chuck wagon—with cooking gear and a store of such food as canned vegetables and dried fruit. The Dutch oven, the "all-purpose" cooker so to speak, perfectly suited both the frying and baking needs of the camp cook and so was his primary tool. Not surprisingly, cheap and plentiful beef, both from the herd and from stray cattle found along the drive, served as the staple ingredient. The cook sometimes served up bacon, which could be dried and carried along in the wagon,

and which the cowboy enjoyed as a nice change of pace from beef every now and then.

For as long as the buffalo still roamed, cowboys also hunted with great pleasure and enjoyed the fresh meat immensely. James Childers described what cowboys ate during a three-month roundup in western Oklahoma in the 1860s: "Buffalos were still existing in rather large numbers during my stay in No-Man's-Land, and we ate a lot of buffalo meat of the choice cuts." Within about a decade, though, hunters had slaughtered

Below: *Always plenty of beans in every cowboy meal. Oklahoma City, Oklahoma, 2004.*

Opposite: *Preparing sourdough biscuits at a chuck wagon gathering in Oklahoma City, Oklahoma, 2004.*

most buffalo for their hides, which they turned into coats and rags. Buffalo remained absent from the cowboy's diet for the next century, until Ted Turner and other entrepreneurs created a buffalo meat "revival" during the late twentieth century.

Wyoming poet Myrt Wallis summed up the cowboy's preferred diet well in her 1995 poem "The Cook."

> *She filled them up on biscuits*
> *Steak and spuds and chili, too*
> *Lemon pie and chocolate cake*
> *Cornbread, beans and good beef stew.*

Born in Texas in 1870, W. H. Thomas fondly recalled meals eaten during his cowboying days. "Eating around a chuck wagon is the best eating in the world. Nothing special, but good solid food like whistle berries [beans], beef, sow belly strips, and some of the best sop in the world can be made from the grease you get from fried sow belly." The cook also baked fruit pie two or three times a week. Mrs. Jack Miles, who rode on roundups in central Texas during the early twentieth century, described a typical roundup meal of fried calf meat or broiled calf ribs, served with garlic chili beans and biscuit bread, and followed up with stewed dried apples and molasses. She also recalled a popular dish amongst cowboys, the so-called "son-of-a-gun." This dish (which also carries a more colorful, vulgar name) included the meat of an unweaned calf, sweetbreads, marrow gut, kidneys, heart, liver, tongue, and brains. Flour thickened the stew, while chilies and onions added zest. As Western historian Ramon Adams

Coffee pot hanging over campfire, Chuck wagon gathering, Oklahoma City, Oklahoma, 2004.

observed, "You throw everything in the pot but the hair, horns and holler."

Beef might have been the staple ingredient in a cowboy's diet, but most any cowboy would agree that it wasn't the most important part of his meal. A three- to five-gallon coffee pot hung over a fire most of the time, and the cowboys demanded hot, strong "brown gargle" with every meal. In *Western Words*, Ramon Adams disclosed the "secret recipe" for what cowboy W. H. Thomas called "the blackest coffee that can be made": The cook boiled the beans for a couple of hours, after which he would "toss in a horse shoe. If the shoe sinks, it ain't ready to drink." If the cook did a good job, the hands might thank him for the "six-shooter coffee," strong and thick enough to float a six-gun. In contrast, weak, watery "belly wash" would bring cries of derision.

In 1865, just in time for the cowboy's heyday, Pittsburgh, Pennsylvania grocers John and Charles Arbuckle created a roasting and coating technique that kept coffee beans tasty for long periods. They concocted a special egg and sugar glaze that sealed in the flavor of their Arbuckle's Ariosa coffee. Before that time, ranchers had to buy green beans and roast them in a skillet, a time-consuming chore that often yielded charred coffee beans. Thus, for the cowboy, Arbuckle's became synonymous with coffee.

Perhaps the most important character trait in any cowboy was his sense of humor. The difficult, demanding nature of his job necessitated a certain calm, laid-back approach to his work if he was to succeed and remain sane. Lucky for him, there were many opportunities for cowhands to "let off steam." The cowboy seized most of them, whether in the city, on the ranch, or out on the plains.

Trail drives presented a special challenge to having fun. The cowboy found himself far from most "civilized" entertainment venues for a long stretch of time. He was at work for weeks on end, and even when he sat down by the campfire to have his meal or tell a tale, a sudden stampede might force him back on the job at any moment. Cowboys therefore invented ways to combine their work with their relaxation, and even used the one to make the other easier.

Singing is a prime example. Cowboys sang just for the fun of it, as Mabel Luke Madison tells of those hired for roundups at the Madison ranch in New Mexico: "After they'd leave, I could hear them singing in the distance: 'Oh, I want to be a cowboy and with the cowboys stand, Big spurs upon my boot-heels, A lasso in my hand.' They had good voices too and just seemed to put their hearts and souls into music." Cowboys also used song to calm the cattle, though, and a stampede was often prevented in this way. Driving and controlling animals posed the central problem on those epic drives, and cowboys had to be inventive to manage semi-wild Longhorns. They made sounds to reassure the herd of human presence and to help prevent a sudden sound from startling the animals. A cowboy might chant snatches of hymns or string together random phrases of profanity. Hardy Jones, of San Angelo, Texas, recalled a typical night's herding in the early 1880s: "At night four boys generally rode herd, two traveling around one way and two the other way. I couldn't sing but I did whistle. I don't know that it helped quiet the steers any but it was better to have some noise, for if every thing was quiet and a sudden noise was made, every old steer jumped up and began to snort."

As far as formality is concerned, a trail drive is a far cry from the office, and cowboys made themselves at

home with their work, with their fellow cowhands, and even with the cattle. They found special pleasure in creative profanity and—in the absence of ladies and far from Victorian social restrictions—enjoyed incorporating it into just about every facet of daily life. Many old-time cowboy songs and poems (since sanitized) featured a strong dose of humorous vulgarity. One popular old ditty carried the title, "The Whorehouse Bells Were Ringing," from which one can imagine the lyrics. African-American cowboy Bones Hooks described the common cowboy pastime of attaching nicknames to most objects and people: "Every horse, every man, bread and other articles of the camp, had a nickname, often unmentionable in mixed groups."

Contrary to yet another myth, most cowboys in the American West could read and write. The stereotype of the unlettered barbarian is refuted by the historical record time and time again, in letters, diaries, and autobiographies written by cowboys and -girls, many of whom had a real way with words. Cowboys simply didn't waste those words on outsiders, and it was outsiders—largely hostile observers from the East—

Jack Rhodes, Sr. playing guitar in Pitchfork bunkhouse at night. Photographed by Charles J. Belden circa 1920s.

Above: *William T. Borron playing the fiddle, 1941.*

Opposite: *Cowboys playing cards, circa 1953.*

that popularized and perpetuated that unfortunate misconception. Among "insiders," many cowboys expressed themselves in very vivid, creative ways. The cowboy's sense of humor is probably the best example of his linguistic capacity, if only because he joked so much. In a letter written on January 23, 1924, cowboy artist Charles M. Russell even described a serious illness with amusing imagery: "I have been layed up with siatic rumitisum for six months. I been near enough Hell to smell smoke." In another letter, written to fellow artist Will James on May 12, 1920, Russell makes light of the injuries that are part and parcel of cowboying: "I never got to be a bronk rider, but in my youthfull days wanted to be, and while that want lasted, I had a fine chance to study hoss enatimy [horse anatomy] from under and over."

Cowboys prided themselves on their droll sense of humor, and those who bothered to get to know them a little usually learned to appreciate it as well. A writer for the *Denver Tribune-Republican* (October 31, 1886) commented that "[c]owboys as a class are brimful and running over with wit, merriment, good humor. They are always ready for a bit of innocent fun, but are not perpetually spoiling for a fight, as has so often been said of them."[27] Ike

Blasingame noted in his book, *Dakota Cowboy*, "I think it must've been born in cowboys to like a good joke."[28]

Cowboys often exhibited a sense of modesty in their wry humor, poking fun at themselves and their admittedly exceptional way of life. Cowgirl poet Georgie Sicking captured the sentiment well in her poem "To be a Top Hand:"

This cowboy looked at me and said
With a sort of a smile,
'A sorry hand is in the way all the time,
A good one just once in a while.'

Even the awareness of how outsiders viewed the cowhand just gave him one more good opportunity to laugh at himself. Pete Clausen, of Mission, South Dakota, told a favorite joke of old-time cowboys. The incident, he claimed, took place during a roundup on the Black Hills Trail. "We were tending our herds when a buggy, occupied by a preacher, his wife and small daughter, drove up. The daughter, after looking around carefully, turned to her mother and said, 'Do cowboys eat grass like the rest of the cattle?' 'No,' her mother answered. 'They're part human.'"[29]

Now and then, the cowboy had his chance to strike back at the outsider—but he never really did any

harm. The playful cowboy simply targeted new hands or a tenderfoot from the East for a little innocent entertainment. Alabama-born Tom J. Snow and many other hands confirmed that there were rites of passage inflicted on all new hands. "One of the favorite tricks of the cowhand was to put a greener [new hand] on a bucking horse and tell the fellow the animal was a good saddle [easy to ride]." Mrs. Jack Miles recalled how hands on her ranch treated inexperienced and/or inept newcomers. "The boys would bend him over the wagon tongue and hit him six or eight licks with a pair of leather leggings. They called that 'putting the leggings on him.' If there was a creek near by, they would throw him in, cloth[e]s and all and tell him to swim or drown." Texas-born Calvin Roberson offered other examples of what amounted to cowboy hazing. "Yellowjackets were put in their beds and cockleburs in their boots. They would leg 'em, get 'em drunk and duck 'em but never really hurt 'em. That was their idea of fun and if a guy come through without too much kickin' he was called good and soon became one of the boys."

"Making a tenderfoot dance." Staged photograph depicting "the traditional cowboy dancing lesson." Photographed by Solomon D. Butcher, 1889.

Above: *Harry Thair, Jack Rhodes, Sr.,*
Hugh Winsor, Hugh (the horse).
Photographed by Charles J. Belden circa
late 1920s.

Once one of the boys, the hazing just turned to pranks. Mrs. Jack Miles described an entertaining night out on the lonesome trail: "One of the boys could make a hissing sound exactly like a rattlesnake. After they went to bed and got warm, Frank began to hiss through his teeth. The other old boy came out of that bed like a wild cat and could not be persuaded to go back to bed that night."

Today, cowboy poets, singers, and cartoonists perpetuate elements of old-time cowboy humor and add new twists as well. Some new cowboy poems have even already become modern classics. "Reincarnation," by Wallace D. McRae, humorously and creatively compares a cowboy to horse manure. "The Oyster," by Baxter Black, depicts a culture clash between an eastern woman and a cowboy: she is talking about oysters from the sea, but he is imagining "mountain oysters" (fried calf or lamb testicles, a Western delicacy). A legion of artists and cartoonists, including Paul Crites, "Mad Jack" Hanks, Walt LaRue, Ace Reid, and Bonnie Shields, create comic images of cowboy life. For more than 25 years, the singing group "Riders in the Sky" has combined excellent musicianship and harmonious singing with zany humor. The group consists of Ranger Doug ("Idol of American Youth"), Woody Paul ("King of the Cowboy Fiddlers"), Too Slim ("A Righteous Tater"), and Joey ("The CowPolka King").

Since there have been cities in the Wild West, cowboys have been seeking entertainment in them. Spanish and Mexican vaqueros reveled in the wide variety of fun recalled by Casad Humboldt in Mesilla, New Mexico, during the 1870s. In addition to bullfights, he enjoyed "cock fights, bowling alleys, fiestas and street fairs. Saloons, of course, gambling houses, billiard halls, and theaters. Those were exciting days." Above the sounds of the hustle and bustle of street commerce, he recalled "the sing-song voices of venders crying, 'tamales, tortillas, dulcies [candy]!'"

Below: *"Cowhand at dance." Photographed by Arthur Rothstein in Birney, Montana, June 1939.*

Above: *Long Branch Saloon, Dodge City, Kansas, 2001.*

Opposite: *Boot Hill Jail, Dodge City, Kansas, 2001.*

The exploits of inebriated cowboys fresh off the trail helped establish the negative reputation so often attributed to them. Many eastern journalists, having never ridden on a trail drive, only witnessed cowboy antics in town. "A very rough town" is how R. P. Vann, of Webbers Falls, Oklahoma, described the town of Muskogee in his day. "I have seen a great many fights there and killings were very frequent." City fathers throughout the West understood from experience that ornery cowboys fresh from the range—armed with guns and full of liquor—often caused distress, destruction, and even death. Many Western towns passed gun confiscation laws as a result: a cowboy would deliver up his firepower at the city limits and pick it up again only upon departure. A host of other "special" restrictions could then be expected in town. Vann described two hotels in that "rough town" of Muskogee: "The cowboys always stayed at Strokey's place as they did not like to go to Mitchell's hotel, because Mitchell did not like to have them go to bed with their boots on. Strokey was not so particular, and there they could get drunk and sleep with their boots on."

Most cowboy fun, however, involved more peaceful pursuits than shooting up the town and threatening the local citizenry. Winter fun might be ice skating or ice fishing in the Dakotas. In south Texas, people danced the night away at fandangos. Holidays and special events, such as county fairs, galas, and dances, would also bring cowboys to town. A correspondent for *Harper's Weekly* recorded the fun in 1889: "With the advent of Christmas the cow-boys from the surrounding ranches gather in the frontier towns. They come on their most fiery horses, and are dressed in their characteristic picturesque costumes. When they have taken drink enough to become boisterous, there follows the reckless riding and the shouting. They are ever ready for a race, and in the Indian country they sometimes match the speed of their horses with their red brothers of the plains."

Below: *Ray Bell competing in Wild Steer Riding event. Photographed by Ralph R. Doubleday, circa 1935.*

Living as far out as they did, ranch people had to create their own entertainment more often than they could make it into town. Many loved to gamble on horse races, cards, and other amusements. Ranch parties and socials, to which a ranch-owning host would invite the surrounding ranching families and their workers, provided the opportunity to pool resources and break free from frontier isolation. Holidays were always a good excuse for a get-together. Laura Iversen Abrahamson described her family's 4th of July gathering on their South Dakota ranch in 1895:"We had swings and hammocks and played games and had lemonade and cake and had so much fun at the picnic that I guess I'll feel all right even if I don't go to anything now for a long time."

BEA KIRNAN TRICK RIDING TRIANGLE RANCH, (DOUBLEDAY) RODEO.

After a long day in the saddle, dances were an especially popular way to relax. Frontier demographics also made them especially problematic, though. Texas-born R. L. Maddox, who began working in Runnels County, Texas, in the early 1880s, recalled just one such problem at a dance near Paint Rock: "Sometimes, and this was one of them, when we were short of girls and wanted to dance a square, some of us boys would tie a bandanna around our head or arm and take the place of the Miss." The rare intergender contact meant that cowboys were often reluctant to go home, as well: "The girls all wanted to go home about three o'clock, so we went out and turned their horses loose and danced until after breakfast." Mrs. Jack Miles remembered ranch dances with particular fondness: "Jack and I attended many frontier socials, picnics, fish fries, races and glorious old time square dances, where the fiddle, banjo, and guitar made 'Sally Gooden,' 'Turkey in the Straw,' and 'Pop Goes the Weasel' famous. Thirty or forty miles was not considered a long distance to go on horse back to a dance."

Above: *"Bea Kirnan trick riding Triangle Ranch Rodeo." Photographed by Ralph R. Doubleday in Wichita Falls, Texas, circa 1925.*

OWEN CROSBY BULLDOGGING FORSYTH, MONT.
(DOUBLEDAY)

Above: *"Owen Crosby bulldogging Forsyth Mont." Photographed by Ralph R. Doubleday in Forsyth, Montana, circa 1935.*

Even while at home, ranch people were rarely bored. The great outdoors always provided them with diversions from the hard work of ranching. Mrs. Jack Miles described the fun she had as a young girl, living along the North Concho River in Tom Green County, central Texas: "I could stay in my saddle from morning until night, eat out of the chuck wagon and attend all the square dances for miles around. I hunted and fished and ran races with the dashing *vaqueros*." South Dakota cowhand Pat J. Gallagher recalled a little grown-up cowboy fun, when one night they captured a big frog at a water hole. "Having lots of whiskey, as I say, and feeling generous, some one had the idea of piping a drink into the frog. This was accomplished and repeated to our delight in watching the antics of a drunken frog."[30] Such behavior would have appalled Carry Nation, the Women's Temperance Union, and animal rights advocates, but cowboys on the range worried little about the views and values of distant "civilization."

By the 1920s, modern inventions had arrived even on the remote Western prairies. Ray Holmes remembered the childhood fun of listening to a battery-powered radio: "You could run it three or four hours in the evening, but you couldn't get anything in the daytime. At night, they had plays you wanted to listen to. There was one called *Little Theater Off Times Square,* and we used to listen to *Amos and Andy* and *Fibber McGee and Molly.* Then, on Saturday nights, the old-fashioned fiddlers would come on 'til about midnight."[31] Radios, automobiles, telephones, and later television and computers gradually brought ranch people into easier, more frequent contact with the outside world.

A writer for *Harper's Weekly* reported in December 1889, "The cow-boy has great contempt for any occupation which he cannot perform on the back of a horse. He is vain of his thin, high-heeled boots, which he believes to look fine in the stirrups, and which are wholly unsuited to walk in." While that statement is a bit of an exaggeration—we've just seen how much the cowboy loved to dance and picnic, for example—it is undeniably true that cowboys did enjoy anything they could on horseback, whether for work or pleasure. Rodeo as a popular spectator sport began as competitions between ranch cowboys after roundups and long trail drives. Eager to show off their riding and roping skills, cowboys competed and bet against one another in makeshift events. These early ranch rodeos represented the beginnings of the all-American sport.

In Western towns, finishing a big communal task—anything from completing a trail drive or roundup to opening a new county building—called for a celebration. Visiting frontiersmen and –women competed in a variety of ranch-style tournaments and events, such as roping, branding, racing, and bronc riding. O. M. Ratliff, born at Gideon, Lee County, Texas, in 1880, described a three-day celebration in Midland, Texas. After "barbecue, racing and roping, and bronc riding, and so on, then we'd dance all night. They'd usually pull one about once a month. Women were scarce out there, and the men would bring their daughters and wives and put [them] up at the hotel. Most of the men would have to sleep in the wagon yard."

Promoters in Western towns saw the profit value of formalizing such cowboy competitions and began sponsoring rodeos. Pecos, Texas, hosted a

Opposite: "Possibly Cecil Cornish on rearing Pinto 'Smokey' wearing silver mounted tack serape behind saddle." Photographed by Ralph R. Doubleday circa 1945.

Above: "The Mountain and Plain Festival Association World's Championship Broncho Busting Contest, October 7–8, Denver, 1902." Denver Lithograph Company, Denver, Colorado.

Above: Rodeo at Fort Worth Stockyards, Texas, 2001.

rodeo in 1883, with Prescott, Arizona, and Cheyenne, Wyoming, following suit in 1887. After a July 4th, 1909 rodeo, organizers in Pendleton, Oregon, decided to make their "Round-Up" an annual event.

From 1883 through 1913, William F. "Buffalo Bill" Cody's Wild West Show entertained crowds across the nation and in Europe. According to one of his programs, people should see his show "because it is a LIVING PICTURE OF LIFE ON THE FRONTIER. You will see INDIANS, COWBOYS, and MEXICANS as they live." Cody well embellished those lives, however, and his genius for showmanship, drama, and costuming influenced rodeo promoters and performers, who in turn livened up their acts. Over time, rodeo events were standardized to include bareback riding, calf roping, saddle bronc

riding, steer wrestling (bulldogging), team roping, bull riding, and women's barrel racing.

Some of those standardized, "livened up" events were not carry-overs from ranch work and fun. Bill Pickett (1870?–1932), a Texas-born cowboy credited with the invention of the rodeo sport of bulldogging, worked as a cowboy and bronc buster in central Texas. One day Pickett noticed a bulldog grabbing a cow by the lower lip and thus controlling the much larger animal. Pickett reasoned that he could do the same thing. He learned to ride up next to a steer, jump from his horse, grab the animal by the horns or neck, and sink his teeth into the animal's lip. Beginning in 1907, he performed this feat for pay with the famous 101 Ranch Wild West Show. For a decade, he wowed

Above: *Oklahoma's Cattlemen's Association Range Round-Up, Lazy E Arena, Guthrie, Oklahoma, 2004. Twelve teams from Oklahoma's largest and most historic ranches compete in six events that represent a combination of the tasks a working cowboy might perform every day. The events are: saddle bronc riding, cattle doctoring, wild cow milking, team branding, team penning, and wild horse racing.*

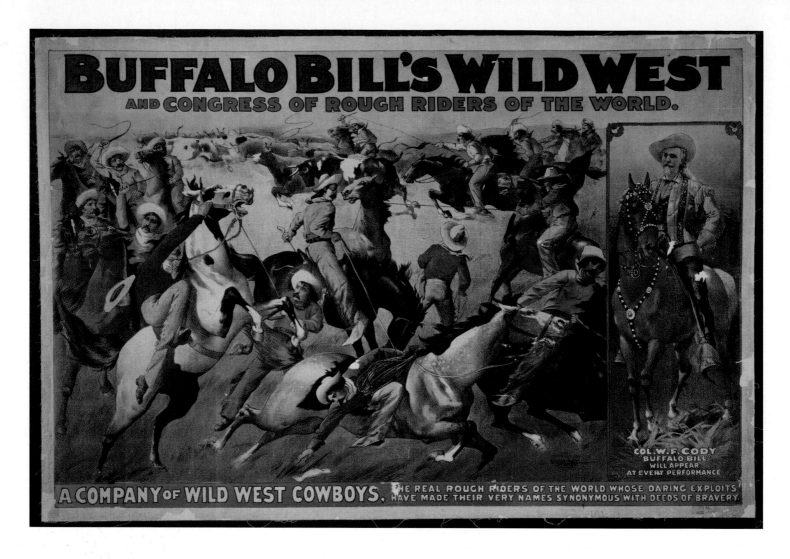

BUFFALO BILL'S WILD WEST
AND CONGRESS OF ROUGH RIDERS OF THE WORLD.

A COMPANY OF WILD WEST COWBOYS, THE REAL ROUGH RIDERS OF THE WORLD WHOSE DARING EXPLOITS HAVE MADE THEIR VERY NAMES SYNONYMOUS WITH DEEDS OF BRAVERY.

COL. W. F. CODY
BUFFALO BILL
WILL APPEAR
AT EVERY PERFORMANCE

Above: *"Buffalo Bill's Wild West and Congress of Rough Riders of the World." Advertising poster from around 1899.*

audiences across the country, even appearing in short films. He continued ranch work from 1916 until his death from a horse's kick in 1932.

Until male competitors marginalized them in the 1930s, some women competed in rough stock events. A "woman steer roper" competed in Cheyenne in 1910, and Fox Hastings competed in the bulldogging competition in Houston, Texas in 1924. "In bulldogging," she said, "you don't tackle two steers exactly alike; you have to learn the difference in their size, strength, formation of horns, build of neck and shoulder, and a lot of things."

The first record of a riding competition that offered a purse (prize money) points to the 1869 4th of July rodeo in Deer Trail, Colorado. Deer Trail was the final destination of several trails in the region, and one summer day cowboys from the Mill Iron, Camp Stool, and Hashknife ranches met there after their long drives and decided to put their skills to the test. A magazine report described the excitement during Will Goff's ride: "He pulled off his coat, threw his suspenders aside, took a reef in his belt and with one bound landed on the bay's back. Swish and his felt hat whistled through the air and caught the bronco (Spanish for coarse, rough, wild) across the side of the head. The pony pitched violently for fifty yards, making about 30 revolutions

a minute." A Mill Iron cowhand, an Englishman named Emilnie Garden-shire, took top honors, riding a wild Hashknife bronco named "Montana Blizzard."

In 1936, rodeo performers in Boston objected to the total purse being less than the sum of their entry fees. They walked out of Col. W. T. Johnson's rodeo and formed a union, the Cowboy's Turtle Association. Johnson met their demand and put up a purse of $14,000. The union evolved into the Professional Rodeo Cowboy's Association (PRCA), and has grown to a membership of about 10,000 today. Rodeo purses have continued to grow as well. In 2002, the National Finals Rodeo in Las Vegas paid out nearly five million dollars in prize money. In 2002, some 23 million people attended more than 700 PRCA-sanctioned rodeos, with competitors carrying away $35 million in prize money. Forty-seven states and four Canadian provinces host these events. The ProRodeo

Above: *William F. "Buffalo Bill" Cody. Photographed by Anderson, New York, New York, circa 1880.*

FOX HASTINGS
ONLY LADY STEER DECORATOR
CALGARY STAMPEDE
(DOUBLEDAY)

Above: *"Fox Hastings only lady steer decorator Calgary Stampede." Photographed by Ralph R. Doubleday, circa 1935.*

Opposite: *Zack Miller, Jr., son of wild west show performer Zack Miller, Sr., on the floor of an auditorium set up for a performance in Chicago, Illinois, 1929.*

Hall of Fame and Museum of the American Cowboy, located adjacent to PRCA national headquarters in Colorado Springs, Colorado, celebrates the sport and commemorates great competitors, both human and animal.

Since 1920, college rodeos have provided lively competition and training for many future professional performers. From humble beginnings at what is today Texas A&M University in College Station, college rodeo competitions have spread to campuses throughout the West. Forty-four men and eighteen women representing eleven colleges and universities competed in the first inter-collegiate rodeo staged near Victorville, California, in 1939. Cutting horse competitions and *charreada* (Mexican rodeo, also called *charrería*) provide other venues of modern cowboy excitement. In her book *Charrería Mexicana: An Equestrian Folk Tradition*, Kathleen Mullen Sands well described the significance of competitions on both sides of the U. S.-Mexican border: "*Charreada* is the distillation of five centuries

NICHOLS TAKING A SPILL FROM STRANG
(COPYRIGHT 1924. R.R. DOUBLEDAY)

"Nichols taking a spill from 'Stranger'."
Photographed by Ralph R. Doubleday in
Bliss, Oklahoma, 1924.

of Mexican horsemanship, the supreme test of man's dominance over animals and his capacity to perform equestrian feats with style as well as daring and athletic prowess." Not surprisingly, food also plays an important role in cowboy festivities today. Whether beef barbecue at a college rodeo or burritos at a charreada, cowboys still enjoy eating as much as they ever did competing—and the good ol' fashion chuck of course keeps cheering fans hearty, too.

THE COWBOY HERO IN POPULAR CULTURE

Though the golden age of trail drives and open-range ranching ended around 1887 and "real" cowboy life as we know it began its decline, authors, painters, and showmen had already begun providing for the cowboy's immortality beginning in 1880.

232

FRANK LESLIE'S ILLUSTRATED NEWSPAPER.

[JUNE 25, 1867.

BRANDING CATTLE ON THE PRAIRIES OF TEXAS—MIRAGE IN THE BACKGROUND.—From a Sketch by James E. Taylor.—See Page 237.

Still during the cowboy's heyday, pulp fiction, novels, Wild West shows, circuses, and early rodeos began to create and shape the cowboy into America's new Western hero—a hero who, at best, was a glorified, romanticized version of the authentic historical cowboy. From that point on, American culture became increasingly suffused with images of the cowboy and his world and, unrealistic as these images usually were, their popularity and cultural influence has been impossible to ignore ever since.

During the twentieth century, radio, film, and television added new, enduring images to the legend, also frequently idealized. Interestingly, however, the cowboy's popularity has always seemed to be cyclical; that is, his visibility rises and falls with changing social circumstances. For example, the "Roaring Twenties" brought rapid social changes, urbanization, and the proliferation of automobiles and other mechanical gadgets to the nation. As the country rushed into an uncertain future, many people longed for the simplicity of bygone frontier days—and so nostalgically looked back to the legendary cowboy for comfort. Luckily, this rapid change also prompted many Westerners to recall and record their experiences on the old open range, and many of our most wonderful examples of cowboy (and cowgirl) testimonials are from this period.

Whether as an escapist fantasy, a return to tradition, or a celebration of the simplified "black-and-white" worldview, the cowboy, his work, and his world play as important a psychological role as a historical one in American culture. Even politicians have seized upon the cowboy as a convenient icon for a variety of policies and purposes—not least of them Theodore Roosevelt, Ronald Reagan, and George W. Bush. However, the cowboy we most often hear invoked by such figures is, of course, not the real cowboy of history just described, but the idealized American hero created by entertainers and embraced by audiences. Where does this image of the cowboy come from? Let's have a look.

In the beginning of cowboy mythologization,

there was the popular novel: dime novels, pulp Westerns, and of course, the ranch romances. While most people today have heard of and many show great literary reverence for Louis L'Amour, the most popular modern writer of Western novels, the cowboy "literature" of the nineteenth and early twentieth centuries in fact had few literary aspirations. Mostly such publications served merely to satisfy the curiosity of the masses of eastern "tenderfoots" about the dangerous and exciting life of the frontier. Among the most popular authors in their own day were Max Brand ("King of the Pulps"), Ned Buntline, and Zane Grey.

Around the turn of the nineteenth century, as real working cowboys began to mourn the loss of the open range, cowboy autobiographies and memoirs became popular reading as well. While these works dispelled the myth that all cowboys were illiterate (in fact, the large majority of them read and wrote quite well), they also tended to reinforce the perception that the cowboy was a hopeless teller of tall tales. Works such as Will James' *Cow-boy Life in Texas* (1893) and Andy Adams' *The Log of the Cowboy* (1903), while unquestionably entertaining, were more a blend of fact, fiction, folklore, and wit than serious and reliable histories.

One of the most interesting cowboy novel "scandals" of all time was that surrounding "Deadwood Dick," probably the most mythologized black cowboy in American history. In 1877, Edward Lytton Wheeler

published the first pulp novel starring a hero by that name. He followed up with over thirty more pulp novels in the eight years between that first publication and his death in 1885. In one tale, the hero interrupts a badman abusing a women: "The next instant Carrol Carner found himself lying at full length upon the ground, while over him stood a handsome fellow in sportish dress—valiant Deadwood Dick."

After Wheeler's death, many men, including Richard Clark, Dick Cole, and Robert Dickey, claimed to be the model for the pulp hero—the real Deadwood Dick. An ex-slave, born in Tennessee or Ohio in 1854, also claimed to be Wheeler's inspiration in his 1907 autobiography, *The Life and Adventures of Nat Love, Better Known in the Cattle Country as "Deadwood Dick"*. Love related his supposed adventures in typical Western tall-tale fashion, with stories of his brave, heroic deeds at

every turn. He claimed to have earned his nickname by winning a roping contest in 1876 in Deadwood, Arizona. Logic would dictate that the much more famous Deadwood, South Dakota, served as Wheeler's inspiration. Given his fanciful self-promotion and exaggerations (like those of all the other claimants to the title), we will probably never know where fact left off and fancy took over in Love's account. He did, however, record a sound version of the cowboy's code: "There a man's work was to be done, and a man's life to be lived, and when death was to be met, he met it like a man."

The popularity of cowboy art, just like other forms of cowboy popular culture, rises and falls depending upon societal trends. The first burst of huge popularity in cowboy art began at the turn of the twentieth century; the latest began in the 1980s and is still going strong, with general interest and avid collecting showing no signs of abating any time soon. However, cowboy art sets itself apart from the literary genre in its faithfulness to reality. Traditionally, both painting and sculpture aspired to represent authentic moments in ranch life. True, many artists added a dash of romance or heightened drama, but all in all artists strived to accurately portray real horses, cattle, equipment, landscapes, and clothing.

Throughout the nineteenth century, it was primarily the vast, rugged Western landscape and its inhabitants that captivated artists. The earliest Western artists, such as George Catlin (1796–1872), Swiss-born Karl Bodmer (1809–1893), and Alfred Jacob Miller (1810–1874), focused on the colorful and exotic elements of Native American life. English-born James Walker (1819–1889) knew Mexican life firsthand and produced richly detailed paintings of vaquero life in California. Others, including Thomas Hill (1829–1913), Albert Bierstadt (1830–1902), and Thomas Moran (1837–1926), focused on the land, painting romanticized visions that tried to convey the grandeur and

Opposite: *Irene Dunne as Sabra Cravat and Richard Dix as Yancey Cravat in the 1931 version of the film* Cimarron.

Below: *John Wayne in* The Big Stampede. *Photographed by John Singer, circa 1932.*

majesty of the West's mountains and valleys.

The cowboy hero on canvas and in bronze wasn't really born until just after the Civil War, though, as the golden age of cattle drives and open-range ranching was dawning. At that time, the conflicts between cavalry soldiers and Indians that followed the war became one of the major themes in Western painting, and works depicting these scenes remain some of the most famous today. New York-born Charles Schreyvogel (1861–1912), in addition to Native American life and cowboys, painted such cavalry charges. Frederic Remington (1861–1909) actually rode with the troops and recorded memorable, romanticized images of frontier battles. At the same time, the sudden phenomenon of trail drives northward from Texas—and the resulting action and adventures in cowtowns—attracted the eye of Remington and other artists.

Remington, who is often granted the title of the greatest cowboy artist of all time, produced a wide range of cowboy drawings, paintings, and later sculpture. His paintings well communicated his nostalgia for the quickly vanishing "Old West" to huge audiences who viewed his works in original form, in magazines, and in reproductions. Describing a roundup for *Collier's* magazine in 1899, he expressed this nostalgia in words: "It is altogether likely the people of the next generation will see nothing of this picturesque and interesting activity."

Remington's main rival, Charles Marion Russell (1864–1926), left his native Missouri as a teenager to work as a cowboy in Montana. During the late 1880s, he increasingly turned his attention to sketching, painting, and modeling small clay figures—sometimes in exchange for a drink at the bar. Even the early works of this self-taught artist revealed a keen eye for observation, an excellent ability to realistically portray animals and humans in action, and a wry sense of humor. Like many of his peers, Russell combined a quest for authenticity with close attention to—and a wistful romanticism for—what he perceived as a vanishing way of life for Native Americans and others on the Western frontier.

The young Russell combined several virtues that served his art career well. An affable sort, he made

Left: A Bad Hoss, *by Charles M. Russell. Circa 1905 reproduction of a 1904 painting.*

Right: Cowboy on a bucking bronco, *by Frederic Remington, circa 1908.*

friends readily and remained loyal to them. In 1896, Russell married Nancy Cooper, whose shrewd business sense and ambition helped catapult him to national fame. And so, when Remington died in 1909, leaving a huge market opening, Russell was ready and quickly filled it. His one-man show at a New York gallery in 1911, followed three years later by an exhibition in London, brought him a wide audience and greatly enhanced the value of his works.

At the dawn of the twentieth century, many other painters were also contributing important paintings documenting cowboy life. Around this time, magazines and journals began taking a more intense interest in life on the frontier, and so these publications became a forum for many cowboy artists' work, particularly illustrations. Like Remington, Frank Tenney Johnson (1874–1939) drew illustrations for magazines and novels and also painted. He developed a particular genius at rendering horses accurately and at depicting the subtle shadings of night scenes. Another artist, W. Herbert Dunton (1878–1936), developed into a fine painter of cowboy life while growing up in the decidedly non-cowboy country of Maine. Beginning about 1896, he traveled to Montana and other Western locations, working as a ranch hand and studying his craft. His realistic illustrations graced many magazines, including *Harper's* and *Scribner's.*

Massachusetts-born N. C. Wyeth's (1882–1935) first painting, *Bronco Buster*, adorned the cover of *The Saturday Evening Post* in 1903, and he became one of the most sought-after illustrators thereafter, his works appearing in nearly every "big-name" journal of his day. Harold von Schmidt (1893–1982), a Californian, illustrated for leading national magazines during the 1930s and '40s. Of his work as a Western artist, he recalled: "I had a chance to be with Indians, to take part in trail drives and to get to know cattle and horses as a working cowboy." Von Schmidt's work replicated the epic style of Remington, in consonance with his stated

Left: *Gary Cooper and Loretta Young in* Along Came Jones, *photographed by John Springer, circa 1945. In* Along Came Jones *(1945), Gary Cooper's character says, "You gotta look like you're somebody and act like you're somebody. Like you can take care of yourself no matter what happens."*

reasoning, with which so many cowboy artists would have agreed: "Our job is to tell the truth as we know it—beautifully and yet forcefully."

Many Western artists who worked around the turn of the twentieth century were trained by master illustrator Howard Pyle, and so they knew one another. Pyle's students included Wyeth, Harvey Dunn, Frank Schoonover, Maynard Dixon, W. H. D. Koerner, and others. Maynard Dixon (1875–1946) worked as a cowboy in the Southwest and painted from his own experience. W. H. D. "Big Bill" Koerner (1879–1938), born in Germany, did not live in the West until the last dozen years of his life. Despite his lack of firsthand observation, he researched

other materials and presented realistic slices of cowboy life. Another student of the Howard Pyle School, John Clymer (1907–1989), was a photorealist painter who paid so much minute attention to detail that his paintings are considered a good substitute for full-color photographs. Tom Ryan (1922–), Harry Jackson (1924–), and Newman Myrah (1921–) perpetuated this photorealist legacy, albeit tinged with romanticism.

Like Western fiction and history, cowboy painting long suffered the criticism and derision of high-brow eastern cultural critiques. Today, however, cowboy images ride through major museums throughout the country and the world. Gordon Snidow, Gary Morton,

Below: *Actor Paul Newman leans against the tail fin of a pink 1958 Cadillac in his role as a ruthless, charismatic rancher in Martin Ritt's 1963 film* Hud, *photographed by Bradley Smith, circa 1962. Paul Newman as Hud philosophizes "Happens to everybody. Horses, dogs, and men. Nobody gets out of life alive."*

Willie Matthews, and Tim Cox, for example, continue the tradition of faithfully depicting cowboy life. Of his own work as a cowboy, Morton noted, "I loved those cowboy days so much that I had to paint 'em for others to enjoy." Cox, from a fourth-generation New Mexico ranching family, says: "To be there on the ranch, to be part of the day, feel the sun, breathe the dust, ride with the cowboys and help them along is what gives feeling to my art. I don't just paint somebody's account of ranch life, second hand." The Cowboy Artists of America, founded in 1964, has been growing at a rapid rate ever since its founding and holding annual exhibitions since 1966. Membership in the pres-

Above: The First Bulldogger, *by Lisa Perry, Fort Worth, Texas. In 1971, Bill Pickett, a famous black cowboy and the first bulldogger, became the first black cowboy to be inducted into the National Cowboy Hall of Fame.*

tigious organization is by selection only, and it is the highest achievement an artist of Western themes can achieve today.

While many artists remain true to representational art, modern cowboy art is more diverse than in the past. Women, Hispanics, and African-Americans appear as artists and subjects much more frequently. For example, José Cisneros (1910–), of El Paso, Texas, has produced an impressive corpus of pen-and-ink drawings that capture the vaquero and other elements of Hispanic life in the West. A large bronze statue of African-American bulldogger Bill Pickett in action now stands in the Fort Worth Stockyards in Texas. In her drawings, Ruth Deoudes (1961–) commemorates the animals, children, and events of ranch life today, and Texas-born Donna Howell-Sickles (1949–) creates whimsical cowgirl paintings. Of her very first inspiration, Howell-Sickles remembers: "I had, as a child, along with the rest of America's children in the 50's, pretended to be that western hero racing across the plains on some inspired mission. Those childhood memories left the Cowgirl image feeling both real and invented and that hint of reality layering appealed to me."

While art and literature are enjoying general popularity these days, a larger, more active Western cultural boom began in the mid-1980s, initiated by the Elko, Nevada, Cowboy Poetry Gathering. That gathering remains a well-attended annual event, but since it got things started, cowboy poetry gatherings, music, museum and rodeo attendance, sales of collectibles, and Indian powwows are also at all-time highs—and show few signs of flagging. Hundreds of cowboy and cowgirl poets now perform at a host of events each year, a handful of whom have achieved national and even international notoriety.

When it comes to zany cowboy humor, "one-time large animal veterinarian" Baxter Black reigns as number one. Many of his poetic works, including *"Vegetarian's Nightmare"* and *"The Oyster,"* express the cowboy's cultural clashes in hilarious fashion. In a more serious vein, Montana rancher and poet Wallace D. McRae takes on weighty issues, like the devastation of the Western landscape through strip mining and other destructive environmental practices. In addition to writing delightful new works, many poets have worked to bring earlier classics to today's audiences. Thus, works by early twentieth-century poets, including S. Omar Barker, Charles "Badger" Clark, Curly Fletcher, Gail Gardiner, and Bruce Kiskaddon, are again being enjoyed. Cowgirl poets are also hard at work, including Linda Hussa, Jane Morton, and Debra Coppinger Hill. Many of Hill's poems convey the honest realities of ranch life, and she explains that she deliberately tries "to document our lives, get things off [her] chest or share moments of joy." Like Baxter Black, Arizona's Dee Strickland Johnson aka "Buckshot Dot" often writes humorous poems.

Above: *Chuck Milner Band, Oklahoma City, Oklahoma, 2004.*

Cowboy singer Michael Martin Murphey's WestFest shows, presented at many Western venues, provide a genial blend of cowboy and Native American music and culture. The Buffalo Bill Historical Center in Cody, Wyoming, hosts an annual Cowboy Songs and Range Ballads event, drawing hundreds of Western performers. Texas poet laureate and singer Red Steagall likewise serves as a major force in promoting authentic cowboy culture at annual gatherings in Ft. Worth, Texas.

In addition to such formal gatherings, many Western museums have enjoyed a visitor boom and expanded their sites during the past two decades. Foremost is the National Cowboy and Western Heritage Museum in Oklahoma City. The vast site includes cowboy, Native American, and other Western art. It also recognizes outstanding rodeo performers, as well as Western actors, singers, and other artists. The Amon Carter Museum in Ft. Worth, Texas, houses extensive collections of works by Remington and Russell, among others. Established in 1956, the Gilcrease Museum of the

SENSATIONAL AND STARTLING "HOLD UP" OF THE GOLD EXPRESS, BY FAMOUS WESTERN OUTLAWS.

Above: *Theatrical poster for* The Great Train Robbery *created by the Strobridge Lithography Company, Cincinnati and New York, 1896.*

Americas in Tulsa, Oklahoma, likewise features extensive Western art collections. In Kerrville, Texas, one can enjoy contemporary Western art at the Museum of Western Art (formerly the Cowboy Artists of America Museum). The Autry National Center Museum of the American West in Los Angeles has reached far beyond Autry memorabilia to establish itself as a major museum and research center for Western American culture. Likewise, the Buffalo Bill Historical Center in Cody, Wyoming, now includes six major complexes, including natural history, art, firearms, and a fine research library.

With all due respect to the cowboy in literature, art, and song, everybody knows that the cowboy has been made most famous on film and television. More people first meet the cowboy in front of their televisions than in any other place, and the popularity of Westerns on film and television appeals to a much larger segment of the population than cowboy art, novels, or music ever have. Not just the audiences, but even the filmmakers themselves, like writers and artists, have found Western and cowboy themes irresistible. In fact, in many cases, filmmakers got their ideas from literature: Owen Wister's novel *The Virginian* (1902) and Larry McMurtry's *Lonesome Dove* (1985) have both been adapted for and well received on screen. In the late 1950s and early '60s, Westerns even constituted the bulk of prime-time television programming. What explains the allure of this genre both to audiences and to the people making films and television shows?

Since *The Great Train Robbery* (1903) proved that cowboy action could also have a plot, the audience appeal of the Western, like many other genres, rests on the surety of good battling and defeating evil. Not unlike medieval morality plays, the Western tests a hero, often against great odds, and he meets the challenge and rights the wrongs. In the 1950s and '60s, this guarantee that good would prevail fit well with the Cold War worldview of good versus evil. Television Westerns provided reassurance to Americans frightened by Soviet expansionism, possible nuclear war, and suspected Communist subversion at home. Each week on the television screen, clear, strong, unambiguous heroes, like Marshal Matt Dillon in *Gunsmoke* and the tough, dependable Cartwright family in *Bonanza*, fought for a just cause, often against difficult odds, but always won in the end.

Western films often played a similar role, placing modern fears in a more comfortable cultural context. As film scholar Stanley Corkin has observed, Westerns "defined an important element of the cultural fabric of the Cold War and in doing so contributed in significant ways to what their viewers thought about themselves, their country, and the world."[32] Just as fans of Westerns cheered the hero and jeered the villain, they also accepted uncritically the Cold War morality play vision of the world: America, always right, and the Soviet Union, always evil.

Most viewers today would find the cardboard Western caricatures of the 1950s and '60s juvenile, as well as sexist and sometimes racist. Just like the popularity of other cowboy forms of art, however, the cowboy on screen makes a comeback every now and then, and it's making one—albeit a mod-

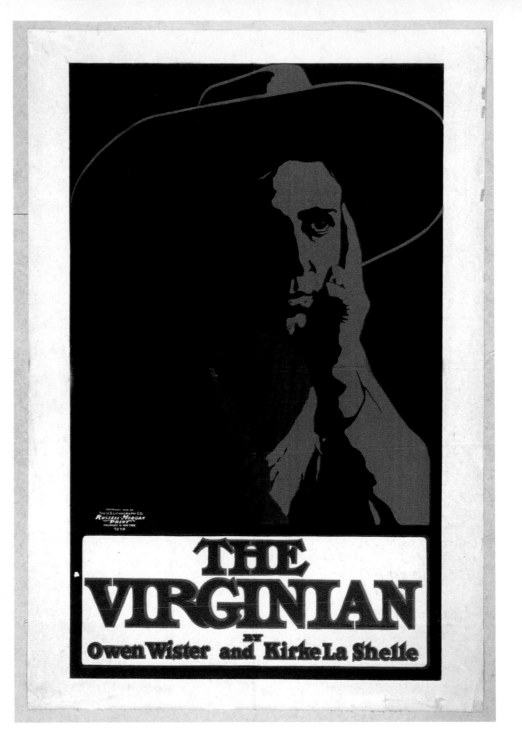

Above: *Theatrical poster for the film* The Virginian, *by Owen Wister and Kirke La Shelle, created by the U.S. Lithograph Company, Russell-Morgan Print, Cincinatti and New York, circa 1903.*

Left: *Cast of* Gunsmoke *on set. From left to right: James Arness as Marshal Matt Dillon, Burt Reynolds as Quint Asper, Ken Curtis as Deputy Festus Haggen, Amanda Blake as Kitty Russell, and Milburn Stone as Galen "Doc" Adams. Photographed between 1964 and 1965.*

Right: *Cast of* Bonanza *on horseback. Lorne Greene (center) played Ben Cartwright, father of three grown sons. Michael Landon (left) and Dan Blocker (right) played Little Joe and Hoss, respectively, two of the Cartwright boys. Photographed between 1962 and 1970.*

est one—today. Through most of the 1990s, few Westerns appeared on television. Hollywood released no cowboy films in 2002, but in 2003, Kevin Costner's well-received *Open Range* brought together a strong cast, a sprightly musical score, and Costner's considerable skill in crafting Western tales. The following year, the Western and cowboys reappeared on television with the production of two new series, HBO's *Deadwood* and *Into the West* on TNT.

Why another Western resurgence now? Well, as different as contemporary Western heroes and plots are from their counterparts of the '50s and '60s, their audience appeal may very well stem from the same psychological and social factors. The cultural roots of recent Westerns certainly run deeper in the post-9/11 United States. General Tommy Franks, for example, who led coalition forces in Operation Iraqi Freedom, admitted that "I like the old Westerns. I'm a corny guy. I like white hats and black hats." Similarly, a comment by "Howard" on the *Washington Monthly* website from October 22, 2004, extended the influence of Westerns to President George W. Bush: "As far as I can tell, Bush has no idea of

'where we need to go,' he just has an idea, based on TV Westerns of the '50s, that this is a struggle between white hats and black hats." Journalist Christopher Corbett aptly summed up the Western cultural resurgence: "[Westerns] may very well be on the upswing right now for lots of reasons, 9/11 included. But I think mainly that the West is just powerfully alluring. It is remembered as a simpler time when a man's best hope, and sometimes his only hope, was himself."

Add to this comforting worldview galloping hoofbeats, exotic dress and locations, gunplay, and fistfights, and you've got some great entertainment with enormous audience appeal. Of course the hero overcomes seemingly impossible obstacles and defeats the villain, and right prevails over wrong. But in addition to this, the traditional B-Western movies were defined by many more formulaic elements that added to their fascination. Plots, such as the "Bob Steele plot," in which the young hero was pitted against murdering outlaws, were typically predictable, frequently centering around missions of retribution and justice. Action, conflict, and humor, not deep character development or extensive dialogue, marked most Westerns. The action itself was usually rendered in the form of ritualized—not graphic—violence. Sidekicks and/or talented horses added humorous touches and magnified the greatness of the hero, and there were often heroines who needed saving (but only the more daring director suggested a hint of chaste love with the cowboy hero).

In spite of the "formulas," all Westerns are certainly not the same. In fact, a central appeal to scriptwriters themselves has always been the Western's almost infinite capacity for adaptation. With the exception of a few films, such as *Monte Walsh* and *Will Penny*, that strived to present the grit and authenticity of cowboy life in the Old West, most Westerns did include some formulaic elements (horses, conflict, heroes, villains, a heroine to be saved, great scenery, etc.). Beyond that, though, any type of plot line could be rendered

Opposite: *A scene from the 1954 film* Johnny Guitar. *Joan Crawford (left) starred as the saloon owner, Vienna; Sterling Hayden (right) starred as Johnny Logan; and Frank Marlowe (background) was the saloon bartender.*

Below: *Close-up of Clint Eastwood in scene from movie* High Plains Drifter.

into a Western format: action, comedy, dramatic conflict, romance. Thus we get singing cowboys, like Roy Rogers and Gene Autry. We get cowboys wielding bullwhips more often than guns, like Lash LaRue and Whip Wilson. The Marx Brothers brought their zany physical humor to the Western. The 1960s brought a rash of "spaghetti Westerns," following the lead of Sergio Leone's directing, Clint Eastwood's acting, and Ennio Morricone's music. George Lucas even took Western themes and figures into outer space with his *Star Wars* films, and future filmmakers will doubtless find still more ways to keep reshaping the traditional Western into new forms.

A certain amount of familiarity was provided by the star system, which developed quickly in Western film and television and formed the genre's central appeal. But again, even these familiar heroes, heroines, villains, sidekicks, and horses came in all types. The steely-eyed William S. Hart, for example, always wore regular cowboy garb and prided himself on fine touches of authenticity in his films. In contrast, Tom Mix and Gene Autry sported elaborately tailored shirts and fancy boots, more akin to drugstore than working cowboys. Loyal fans supported all their various favorites: from the early days of Bronco Billy Anderson, silent stars including Johnny

Mack Brown, Wild Bill Elliott, Hoot Gibson, William S. Hart, Buck Jones, Allan "Rocky" Lane, Ken Maynard, Tom Mix, Audie Murphey, Randolph Scott, Charles Starrett, Fred Thomson, Tom Tyler, and many, many others thrilled fans of all ages and all tastes.

A few cowboy heroes, such as Gary Cooper and Gregory Peck, managed to rise above the B-Westerns to be taken seriously and to appear in bigger-budget, better-publicized, and critically-acclaimed films. Only one actor, however, came to personify the cowboy hero to a legion of fans: John Wayne. Despite nearly half a century of filmmaking and immense audience appeal, he only earned somewhat grudging recognition from professionals of the film industry late in his life. The Duke's collaboration with skillful directors, most notably John Ford and Howard Hawks, produced many successful films, from *Stagecoach* (1939) and *Red River* (1948) to *The Searchers* (1956), *True Grit* (1969), and *The Shootist* (1976). In the latter film, the Duke passed his cowboy code along to a young Ronnie Howard: "I won't be lied to, and I won't be laid a hand on; I don't do these things to other people, and I won't have them do them to me."

A few black cowboys gained a measure of fame and notoriety on the silver screen as well. In the late 1930s, the talented singer Herb Jeffries starred in several films as the world's first black singing cowboy. Perhaps the best example, though, is Bose Ikard, born a slave in Mississippi in 1847. At just five years old, Ikard traveled west to Texas with his master. When the young cowboy was freed by the Civil War just over a decade later, he went to work for

Charles Goodnight and, in 1866, helped Goodnight and his partner Oliver Loving blaze a trail west out of Texas and north into Colorado. Goodnight praised his trusted hand: "He was my detective, banker, and everything else in Colorado, New Mexico, and the other wild country I was in. . . . He surpassed any man I had in endurance and stamina." Ikard and Goodnight both died in 1929. Over half a century later, however, Ikard's life was brought to the attention of a large audience by the Larry McMurtry novel and popular television miniseries *Lonesome Dove*, in which Danny Glover portrayed Ikard as the character Joshua Deets.

Stock villains were invariably booed by fans when they appeared on screen, but such stars as Ted De Corsia, Jack Elam, Jack Palance, and Forrest Tucker were as loved in their roles as many heroes. Their ubiquitous black hats marked them as the bad guys, rendering them famous (or infamous) in their own right. Likewise, a faithful sidekick rode with the hero and further heightened the hero's stature. Throughout a career in radio, film, television, and comic books, the stoic Tonto aided the Lone Ranger and became practically as celebrated as the hero himself. In many cases, slapstick humor marked the sidekick's actions and brought laughs to the audience. Forest "Fuzzy" Knight, Al "Fuzzy" St. John, Pat Buttram, and other funny sidekicks became stars in their own right. After making some forty films, Buttram switched to television, appearing with Gene Autry from 1950–56. Of his old sidekick, Autry said, "He was great, off the film and on the film. . . . If I needed a good one-liner right quick, he would give me a good routine." Lester "Smiley" Burnette, aka "Frog" Millhouse, became well known for working alongside Gene Autry, but

Below: Portrait of husband-wife acting team, Roy Rogers and Dale Evans. Unknown photographer, circa 1955.

he also made films with Charles Starrett and Roy Rogers. George "Gabby" Hayes rode with half a dozen leading stars of the 1930s, before settling in as the toothless and not very intelligent sidekick to Roy Rogers.

Many talented women played cowgirl sidekicks, including Kay Buckley, Gail Davis, Penny Edwards, Mona Freeman, Mary Beth Hughes, Vera Ralston, Linda Stirling, Peggy Stewart, and many more. Women usually served as minor characters in television, again like the old B-Westerns, but they sometimes took more visible and assertive roles in film. Major female stars, beginning with Marlene Dietrich and Mae West, even enjoyed top billing. Barbara Stanwyck, for example, starred in *Annie Oakley* and *Cattle Queen of Montana*. Joan Crawford played a tough, determined cowgirl against an equally tough Mercedes McCambridge in *Johnny Guitar*. Jane Russell's character, Rio, in the Howard Hughes film *The Outlaw*, raised the eyebrows of censors in 1943 and ushered in the adult Western. Only Dale Evans, however, the so-called "Queen of the West," earned consistent equal billing with costar and husband Roy Rogers, both in films and television.

Some B-Western cowboy stars even gave equal billing to their horses. Heroic horses had great audience appeal, especially with children, who love animal stories. A brave, intelligent horse often saved his rider—and the day. Like the sidekick, the hero's horse might inject a note of humor now and then, perhaps giving the hero—ever bashful with women—a nudge in the back that pushes him into the heroine's arms. The Lone Ranger could not face danger without Silver, nor Tonto without Scout. William S. Hart astride Fritz and Fred Thomson on Silver King would surely run down the bad guys, and Tom Mix's Tony and Ken Maynard's Tarzan had nearly as many fans as their masters.

Above: *Over the years, some 18 actors have portrayed the Lone Ranger on radio and television. The first* Lone Ranger *show aired in 1933 on the radio station WXYZ Detroit. In all, 3,500 radio shows, two 15-chapter Republic serials, 221 television segments, and three theatrical releases have been produced, according to the Wrather Corporation, which still syndicates the television series.*

While many of these movie and television formulas can still be found in today's Westerns, modern technology and society have also produced a lot of changes in the genre. Fascination with technology and the search for yet another angle spurred the History Channel's series *Wild West Tech* (2004), which documents the inventions and technology of the Old West. Special effects and digital imaging also mean that stunts can be far more spectacular and violence much more graphic and realistic than in earlier films and television programs. Until HBO's *Deadwood* series (2004), for example, television Westerns were generally relatively tame and predictable, not unlike the old-time B-Western movies and serials. While even these Westerns suffered some criticism, you did not find in them the eulogizing of violence that you saw in Sam Peckinpah's *The Wild Bunch*. Additionally, the cast of characters has broadened to include more ethnic diversity and to give women more prominent roles, as we see in the *Dr. Quinn, Medicine Woman* series, starring Jane Seymour. These days modern audiences also expect great authenticity, right down to horse and cattle breeds, clothing, firearms, and equipment, a demand earlier audiences never would have made.

Even with all the new technologies at work, core values, familiar characters, and predictable plots still appear in most Westerns, and they still appeal to most audiences. After all, no matter what form a Western takes, it still has to have certain characteristics to be recognizable as a Western in the first place. In the best cases, a Western resurgence is kicked off by some creative mind that blows new life and variation into the old formula long after audiences thought it was dead (or done to death, rather). Even after a long absence, though, somebody—creative or not—always seems to "go back to the well" and discover that, lo and behold, the Western wasn't really dead. In fact, like the traditional cowboy hero, the Western never really dies at all. It just rides off into the sunset for a spell.

Original caption: *"01/05/1938. A natural horseman and one of the greatest trick riders to ever appear in motion pictures, Gene Autry, Republic star, is just as much at home on a horse off the screen as on. He is shown here putting "Champion," his favorite mount, through some of his paces. Gene personally raises and trains all of his horses on his own ranch in the San Fernando Valley near Hollywood, California."*

If this book piqued your interest in cowboy life, you'll probably want to know where you can find out more. Which books are good? What museums are there to visit? Where are there cowboy and Western events? Well, pardner, here are some great suggestions for you!

Right from the horse's mouth

To get to the grit and gristle of range life, there's nothing like firsthand reports from working ranch people. On the Internet, go to "American Life Histories: Manuscripts from the Federal Writers' Project, 1936–1940" at http://memory.loc.gov/ammem/wpaintro/wpahome.html. Many of the direct quotations used in this book come from transcripts of those interviews, but there's plenty left to be enjoyed at the site!

Want to read written firsthand accounts? Try:

- 1874. Joseph G. McCoy. *Historic Sketches of the Cattle Trade of the West and Southwest*.
- 1882. John K. Rollinson. *Pony Trails in Wyoming: Hoofprints of a Cowboy and U. S. Ranger*.
- 1885. Charles A. Siringo. *A Texas Cow Boy or Fifteen Years on the Hurricane Deck of a Spanish Pony*.
- 1888. Theodore Roosevelt. *Ranch Life and the Hunting Trail*.

Many of the newspaper quotations in this book come from a wonderful collection gathered by Clifford Westermeier, *Trailing the Cowboy: His Life and Lore as Told by Frontier Journalists*. Published in 1955 by Caxton Printers of Caldwell, Idaho, the book is unfortunately long out of print. If you chance upon a copy at a used bookstore, snap it up for some excellent old-time journalism.

Cowboy memoirs

- 1903. Andy Adams. *The Log of a Cowboy*. (As famous Texas folklorist J. Frank Dobie noted, Adams left "a just and authentic conception of trail men, trail work, range cattle, cowboy horses, and the cow country in general.")
- 1920. Clarice E. Richards. *A Tenderfoot Bride*.
- 1920. George W. Saunders. *The Trail Drivers of Texas*.
- 1934. Mary Kidder Rak. *A Cowman's Wife*.
- 1939. Edward Charles "Teddy Blue" Abbott and Helena Huntington Smith. *We Pointed Them North*.
- 1941. Agnes Morley Cleaveland. *No Life for a Lady*. (J. Frank Dobie called this memoir of New Mexico ranching the "best book on range life from a woman's point of view ever published.")
- 1954. Bert L. Hall, ed. *Roundup Years: Old Muddy to Black Hills*.
- 1958. Ike Blasingame. *Dakota Cowboy: My Life in the Old Days*.
- 1969. Ed Lemmon. *Boss Cowman: Recollections of Ed Lemmon, 1857–1946*.
- 1994. Margot Liberty, Barry Head, and Ray Holmes. *Working Cowboy*.

Museums

- Amon Carter Museum, Ft. Worth, Texas. http://www.cartermuseum.org
- Autry National Center: Museum of the American West, Los Angeles, California. http://www.autry-museum.org
- Buffalo Bill Historical Center, Cody, Wyoming. http://www.bbhc.org
- C. M. Russell Museum, Great Falls, Montana. http://www.cmrussell.org/
- Gilcrease: The Museum of the Americas, Tulsa, Oklahoma. http://www.gilcrease.org
- The Museum of Western Art, Kerrville, Texas. http://www.caamuseum.com/
- National Cowboy & Western Heritage Museum, Oklahoma City, Oklahoma. http://www.nationalcowboymuseum.org
- National Cowgirl Museum and Hall of Fame, Ft. Worth, Texas. http://www.cowgirl.net/
- Sid Richardson Collection of Western Art, Ft. Worth, Texas. http://www.sidrmuseum.org/

Events

- American Chuck Wagon Association. http://www.chuckwagon.org
- American West (calendar of cowboy poetry and song fests). http://www.americanwest.com/pages/events.htm
- Cheyenne Frontier Days, Cheyenne, Wyoming. http://www.cfdrodeo.com/
- Chisholm Trail Heritage Center, Duncan, Oklahoma. http://www.onthechisholmtrail.com/
- Cowboy Songs and Range Ballads, Cody, Wyoming, (hosted by the Buffalo Bill Historical Center). http://www.bbhc.org/events/
- Friends of Rodeo. http://www.friendsofrodeo.com/
- Let's Rodeo (links to lots of rodeo organizations).

http://cyberrodeo.com/guysgals/rodeo.htm
- Michael Martin Murphey's WestFest. http://www.westfest.net/
- National Cowboy Poetry Gathering, Elko, Nevada (organized by the Western Folklife Center). http://www.westernfolklife.org
- National Cowboy Symposium & Celebration and National Championship Chuckwagon Cookoff, Lubbock, Texas. http://www.cowboy.org/
- Pendleton Round-up, Pendleton, Oregon. http://www.pendletonroundup.com/
- The Professional Rodeo Cowboys Association. http://www.prorodeo.org/
- Red Steagall Cowboy Gathering, Ft. Worth, Texas. http://www.theredsteagallcowboygathering.com/
- Western Heritage Classic, Abilene, Texas. http://www.westernheritageclassic.com/
- The Women's Professional Rodeo Association. http://www.wpra.com/
- Working Ranch Cowboys Association. http://www.wrca.org

Play cowboy
- DudeRanches.com. http://www.duderanches.com
- The Dude Ranchers' Association. http://duderanch.org
- Gene Kilgore's Online Guide to Ranch Vacations. http://www.ranchweb.com
- Lone Hand Western by Mark Bridge, PhD (learn to play and sing some cowboy songs). http://www.lonehand.com/

1 *Texas Livestock Journal*, October 21, 1882, reprinted in Clifford P. Westermeier, ed., *Trailing the Cowboy: His Life and Lore as Told by Frontier Journalists* (Caldwell, ID: Caxton Printers, 1955), pp. 42-43.

2 Printed in *Denver Republican*, Colorado, August 7.

3 Ike Blasingame, *Dakota Cowboy: My Life in the Old Days*, 1958 Reprint. (Lincoln: University of Nebraska Press, 1964), p. 241.

4 N. Howard Thorp, Printed in *Songs of the Cowboys*.

5 Margot Liberty and Barry Head, *Working Cowboy: Recollections of Ray Holmes* (Norman: University of Oklahoma Press, 1995), p. 77.

6 Blasingame, *Dakota Cowboy*, p. 200.

7 Reprinted in Westermeier, *Trailing the Cowboy*, p. 103.

8 John K. Rollinson, *Pony Trails in Wyoming: Hoofprints of a Cowboy and U. S. Ranger*, 1941 Reprint (Lincoln: University of Nebraska Press, 1968, 1988), p. 33.

9 Ed Lemmon, *Boss Cowman: Recollections of Ed Lemmon, 1857-1946*, 2002 Reprint ed. Nellie Snyder Yost, introduction by Richard W. Slatta (Lincoln: University of Nebraska Press, 1969), pp. 303-04. On dress, see also Tom Lindmier and Steve Mount, *I See By Your Outfit: Historic Cowboy Gear of the Northern Plains* (Glendo, Wyoming: High Plains Press, 1996).

10 Lemmon, *Boss Cowman*, p. 302.

11 Lemmon, *Boss Cowman*, p. 109.

12 J. Marvin Hunter, ed., *The Trail Drivers of Texas* Reprint (Austin: University of Texas Press, 1985), p. 453.

13 Laura Aleta Iversen Abrahamson, "Herding Cows and Waiting Tables: The Diary of Laura Aleta Iversen Abrahamson," *South Dakota History*, 20: 1 (Spring 1990), pp. 24, 45.

14 Rollinson, *Pony Trails*, p. 135.

15 Lemmon, *Boss Cowman*, p. 229.

16 Printed in *Facts*, Colorado Springs, Colorado. August 19, p. 21.

17 Hunter, *Trail Drivers*, p. 631.

18 Theodore Roosevelt, *Ranch Life and the Hunting Trail*. 1899. Facsimile Edition (Ann Arbor, Michigan: University Microfilms, 1966), p. 24.

19 Hunter, *Trail Drivers*, pp. 238-39.

20 N. Howard Thorp, Printed in *Songs of the Cowboys*.

21 Reprinted in Westermeier, *Trailing the Cowboy*, pp. 97-98.

22 Lemmon, *Boss Cowman*, p. 69.

23 Hunter, *Trail Drivers*, pp. 296-303.

24 Reprinted in Westermeier, *Trailing the Cowboys*, pp. 30-31.

25 Hunter, *Trail Drivers*, pp. 296-303.

26 Holmes, *Working Cowboy*, p. 28.

27 Reprinted in Westermeier, *Trailing the Cowboy*, p. 28.

28 Lemmon, *Boss Cowman*, p. 224.

29 Quoted in Bert L. Hall, ed, *Roundup Years: Old Muddy to Black Hills*, Reprint (Pierre, SD: Western South Dakota Buck-a-roos, 1956, 2000), p. 35.

30 Hall, *Roundup Years*, p. 361.

31 Holmes, *Working Cowboy*, p. 31.

32 Stanley Corkin, *Cowboys as Cold Warriors: The Western and U.S. History* (Philadelphia: Temple University Press, 2004), p. 12.

INDEX

JOHN WAYNE (1)

ACKNOWLEDGMENTS

Penn Publishing gratefully acknowledges the following institutions and individuals for allowing photographs from their collections to be reproduced in this book:

Archivo General de la Nación, Buenos Aires, Argentina 28

Bettman/Corbis 179, 192-193, 195-197, 199, 201

Bradley Smith/Corbis 187

Buffalo Bill Historical Center, Cody, Wyoming 74-75
  Mr. & Mrs. Charles Belden Collection 4-5, 7, 132-139, 141, 145, 154-156, 160

John Springer Collection/Corbis 182-183, 186, 194

Chicago Daily News negatives collection DN-0088666. Courtesy of the Chicago Historical Society 175

Colorado Historical Society, William H. Jackson collection 148-149

Denver Public Library, Western History Collection 66-69, 71-73
  Charles Kirkland 63
  D. F. Barry 77, 122
  Geoffrey Duncan 56
  Nate Salsbury Collection 41-42, 65
  Ralph R. Doubleday 102

Douglas Engle/Corbis 34

Elan Penn 10, 12-13, 22-23, 40, 43-44, 47-51, 53, 79, 82, 112-118, 120, 126-129, 144, 150-151, 153, 160-163, 170-171, 188-189

Glenbow Archives 24, 39

Harvard College Library, Theodore Roosevelt Collection 119

Hubert Stadler/Corbis 30-31
  Kona Historical Collection, Captain Cook, Hawaii 37
  Library of Congress Prints and Photographs Division, Washington D.C. 15, 70, 76, 78, 80, 86, 88-89, 91, 95-97, 99-100, 104-109, 140, 161, 172, 178, 180-181, 184-185, 190-191
  Carpenter Collection 29

Montana Historical Society 84-85, 87, 92-93, 123, 142-143

National Cowboy & Western Heritage Museum, Oklahoma City, OK. 6, 9, 52, 57, 58, 121, 130-131, 169, 173, 198
  Bell Photo 14
  L.E. Crawford Ranch Collection 83, 124-125
  Ralph R. Doubleday Collection 11, 90, 94, 164-168, 174, 176-177
  Ron Bledsoe Collection 54-55, 59-61, 64
  Tom Ryan Papers 46, 101, 103, 146-147, 157

Nebraska Historical Society Photograph Collections 16-21, 81, 98, 110-111, 158-159

Penny Tweedie/Corbis 38

Richard A. Cooke/Corbis 36

Richard W. Slatta 29, 35, 62

Staffen Widsrand/Corbis 26, 27

Stephanie Maze/Corbis 32-33

The University of Texas at Austin, The Robert Runyon Photograph Collection, 06175 courtesy of The Center for American History 45

Yann Arthus-Bertrand/Corbis 25